DECK & PATIO
FURNISHINGS

Seating, Dining, Wind & Sun Screens, Storage, Entertaining & More

MICHAEL R. ANDERSON

COOL
SPRINGS
PRESS
Home and Garden Experts

MINNEAPOLIS, MINNESOTA

Quarto is the authority on a wide range of topics.

Quarto educates, entertains and enriches the lives of our readers—enthusiasts and lovers of hands-on living.

www.quartoknows.com

First published in 2016 by Cool Springs Press, an imprint of Quarto Publishing Group USA Inc., 400 First Avenue North, Suite 400, Minneapolis, MN 55401 USA. Telephone: (612) 344-8100 Fax: (612) 344-8692

quartoknows.com
Visit our blogs at quartoknows.com

Cool Springs Press titles are also available at discounts in bulk quantity for industrial or sales-promotional use. For details contact the Special Sales Manager at Quarto Publishing Group USA Inc., 400 First Avenue North, Suite 400, Minneapolis, MN 55401 USA.

10 9 8 7 6 5 4 3 2

ISBN: 978-1-59186-640-4

Library of Congress Cataloging-in-Publication Data

Names: Anderson, Michael, 1959– author.
Title: Deck and patio furnishings / Michael Anderson.
Description: Minneapolis, MN : Cool Springs Press, an imprint of Quarto Publishing Group USA Inc., [2016] | Includes index.
Identifiers: LCCN 2015041132 | ISBN 9781591866404 (pb)
Subjects: LCSH: Furniture making –Amateurs' manuals. | Garden ornaments and furniture.
Classification: LCC TT195 .A63 2016 | DDC 684.1/8–dc23
LC record available at http://lccn.loc.gov/2015041132

Acquiring Editor: Mark Johanson
Project Managers: Alyssa Bluhm, Madeleine Vasaly
Art Director: Brad Springer
Cover Designer: Jay Smith—Juicebox Designs
Layout: Ryan Scheife
Technical Reviewer: Chris Marshall

Printed in China

ACKNOWLEDGMENTS

Thanks to Mark Johanson and Brad Springer for allowing me the opportunity to work on this project. Also, thanks to Jason Swanson at TTI for supplying tools for the production. Many thanks to the team at *HANDY,* specifically Mike Berger, Larry Okrend, Dan Cary, Jenny Stanley, and Connie Bastyr, who allowed me to hone my skills over a 10-year period at that magazine. My experiences there gave me the skills and insight I needed to make this project happen.

Thanks to Dale Berns at Metro Homes, who through his skill has shown me what real artistry with wood looks like. Thanks also to Mike Tavis for letting me borrow tools, giving me project guidance, and letting me eat his food. Annie Berns and Walter Johnson, thanks so much for allowing me into your beautiful yard.

This publication would not have been possible without the support, encouragement, and love of my daughters, Lizzy and Gracie. I am so proud of you both. Finally, to Doris, the love of my life, my muse, my sage, and my best friend to whom this book is dedicated. Thanks, babe. You're still in my heart and my soul.

CONTENTS

INTRODUCTION

Backyard patios and decks are more than extensions of our homes; they are extensions of our personalities. We customize them to fit our needs, styles, and desires. We relax, entertain, and hold special events in these outdoor living spaces. Some of the most important moments of our lives are played out on patios and decks. So it's no surprise that we are driven to spend so much in time and resources to adorn and customize them.

Retailers understand how we feel about our patios and decks, and they invest in large and varied displays of furniture and decorative accessories in their stores. The entire leisure lifestyle industry has grown into an over $6 billion a year business in the United States. Backyard living no longer means plain resin chairs, a table, and a grill. It's about making a patio or deck a greater part of the home and bringing our indoor comforts and amenities to the outside of the home as well.

As interest in beautifying and expanding our outdoor living spaces continues to grow, so do the creative ways we customize, design, and build our own projects. Outdoor kitchens, fire pits, water features, and pergolas adorn decks and patios, and new ideas are constantly being dreamed up and built by intrepid do-it-yourselfers. At the same time, there is a growing interest in reuse, which works well for building many outdoor projects. A quick search on the Internet will result in a multitude of outdoor furnishings

built from ordinary wood pallets and other recycled materials such as concrete, glass, stone, and tile.

Building projects for your backyard is not only an enjoyable pastime, but it can be economically advantageous as well. The prices for outdoor furnishings can reach seriously elevated levels, so it makes sense to use a combination of materials, skills, and creativity to build your own. Plus, the satisfaction in creating something yourself is highly rewarding. Some projects may even become prized family heirlooms, transcending any monetary value. When people turn to you and ask, "You built that?" or proclaim, "I want one of those," you can take pride in what you've accomplished.

This book offers beginners easy construction techniques to achieve professional-looking results using standard materials and tools. Designed to be functional while

looking refined, the projects in these pages can be modified to suit individual needs. Basic tools are used, and several projects can be constructed using only the simplest of hand tools. The materials are all easily obtainable and are most often standard dimensional lumber. The caveat that dimensional lumber varies in actual size must be stated, but with careful measuring and cutting, you can still get excellent results.

The tools shown are standard and also available at most home centers and hardware stores. All the projects featured can be built with hand and portable tools. Those with more seasoned skills and sophisticated power tools can build these same designs utilizing more advanced construction techniques. Regardless of what your set of tools includes, always think safety first. Know your abilities and

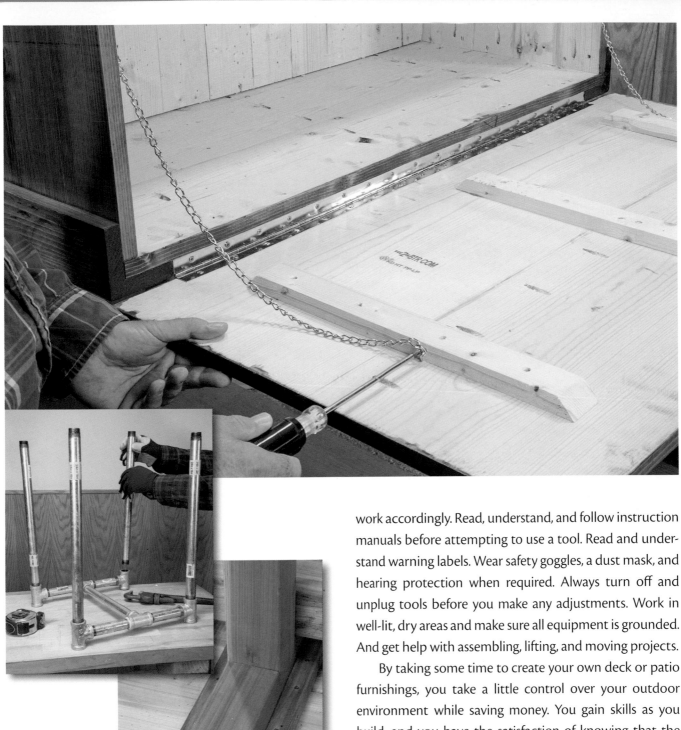

work accordingly. Read, understand, and follow instruction manuals before attempting to use a tool. Read and understand warning labels. Wear safety goggles, a dust mask, and hearing protection when required. Always turn off and unplug tools before you make any adjustments. Work in well-lit, dry areas and make sure all equipment is grounded. And get help with assembling, lifting, and moving projects.

By taking some time to create your own deck or patio furnishings, you take a little control over your outdoor environment while saving money. You gain skills as you build, and you have the satisfaction of knowing that the furnishings you enjoy are one of a kind.

The PROJECTS

PANEL PLANTER

Put your favorite plants on a pedestal to give your deck or patio a visual lift

There are countless ways to build a planter. It is, after all, just a pretty box into which we place our plants. This version is a bit different as it mimics the kind of wood panels typically used in tabletops and other interior furniture. The traditional way of building wood panels requires exacting work, starting with a planer, jointer, and other advanced woodworking tools. This planter design, however, is much simpler by comparison. It uses standard dimensional cedar and mahogany, pocket joinery, and glue. The resulting panels may not be as perfectly smooth and flat as they'd need to be for a dining table, but you can build it in a few hours and get results that look great.

By using contrasting 2 x 4 cedar and 1 x 2 mahogany stock, the panels are striking in appearance. The ribbons of dark mahogany contrast dramatically with the lighter cedar. Choose the best quality lumber you can, looking for the straightest boards. You can cut the lumber into individual lengths, or build one large panel and cut it into sections after construction, as shown on the next page. Whatever method you use, you'll end up with a beautiful planter that will stand out from the usual box.

PANEL PLANTER

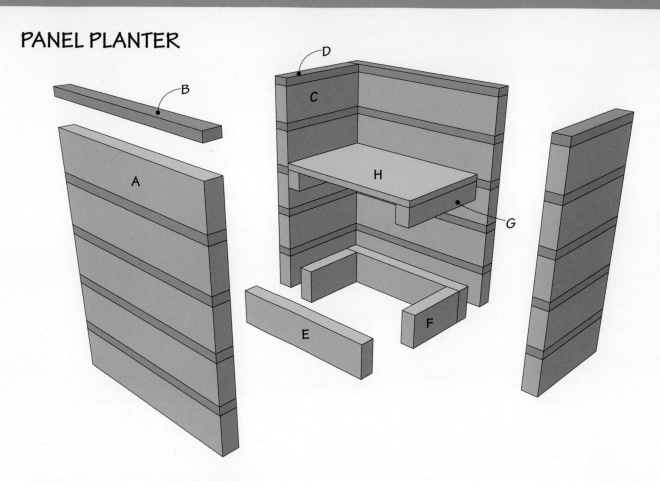

POCKET HOLE LOCATIONS

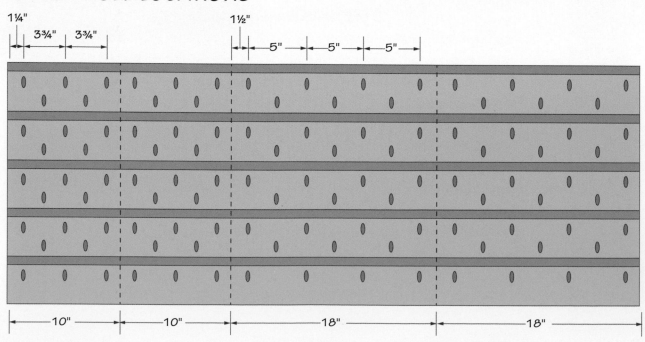

Cutting List

Key	Qty	Description	Size
A	10	Cedar Front/Back	1½ x 3½ x 18 in.
B	10	Mahogany Front/Back	1½ x 1½ x 18 in.
C	10	Cedar Sides	1½ x 3½ x 10 in.
D	10	Mahogany Sides	1½ x 1½ x 10 in.
E	2	Base Front/Back	1½ x 3½ x 15 in.
F	2	Base Sides	1½ x 3½ x 7 in.
G	2	Shelf Supports	1½ x 1½ x 10 in.
H	1	Shelf	¾ x 10 x 15 in.

Materials List

Qty	Description
10	2 x 4 in. x 8 ft. cedar
10	1 x 2 in. x 8 ft. mahogany
	2½-in. stainless-steel pocket screws
	Exterior glue
	Plastic lining (optional)

Tools	
Drill/driver	Saw
Tape measure	Clamps
Square	

Working with Pocket Screws

Pocket screws create butt joints in wood that are practically instant to make and outperform plain butt joints in strength and reliability of alignment. To make them you need an inexpensive clamp-on pocket hole jig (left photo), special drill bit for drilling pocket holes and a long screwdriving bit (middle photo), as well as some self-tapping pocket screws that are designed so the screw head will be recessed below the wood surface when the joint is done (right photo).

How to Build a Panel Planter

(#1) Cut the cedar and mahogany boards to 56 inches. You should be able to locate stock that is sized to the dimensions shown in the cutting list at your local building center or lumber yard. If not, you'll need to purchase random-width stock and use a planer and jointer to dimension it. Drill pocket holes into the top and bottom of the 2 x 4 cedar following the layout diagram in the illustration on page 14.

(#2) Arrange the boards with the 1 x 2 mahogany in between the cedar boards. Apply wood glue (exterior rated) between each layer of wood and then lightly clamp them together. Use scrap 2 x 4s as cauls to clamp the boards down to the work surface, which should be as flat as possible. Use a rubber mallet to help push the boards into place and then tighten the clamps. Drive 2½-inch screws into the pocket holes from both directions and into the mahogany strips. Allow the glue to dry.

Wood caul

(#3) Remove the clamps and lay out cutting lines to divide the glued-up slab into four smaller panels (the front, back, and two sides). Cut the panel along the cutting lines with a circular saw and a straightedge cutting guide.

(#4) Drill pocket holes into the two narrow side panels and then attach them to the front and back panels with 2½-inch pocket screws, forming the box. Take care to make the joints between panels as flush and smooth as you can.

(#5) Attach the 2 x 4 base cleats to the bottom, inside surfaces of the box using more 2½-inch screws. The cleats should extend 1½ inches (and no more) outside of the box panel bottoms to create a "foot" for the box so it rests more stably and limits ground contact with the nicer-quality cedar and mahogany stock. Add a pair of 2 x 2 shelf supports midway up the inside of the box to create a support ledge for the shelf. Cut a shelf from ¾-inch exterior plywood and attach it to the 2 x 2 ledge. Line the box and shelf with plastic and plant it, or just insert a container with plants.

PLANTER BENCH

Refined style, a built-in planter and storage space inside; all made with ordinary 2 x 4s

This stylish bench makes a statement on any patio or deck with its elegant angles and nice proportions. The legs repeat the angled accent of the front and back panels, giving this seating the look of a settee more than that of a bench. Sized so that transporting it is easy, it features a built-in planter opening that can hold a pot of flowers, a thatch of ornamental grass, or even a bonsai display.

An interesting aspect about this design is that it's completely built from 2 x 4 stock. Boards are edge-glued to form panels and are supported by battens that do double-duty as legs. The side panels are set inward from the ends, which highlights the angles. The seating area also includes a lift-off section, allowing storage inside.

This unique bench will look good built from an exotic wood, but is equally attractive when constructed from everyday (and inexpensive) dimensional pine and painted or stained.

PLANTER BENCH

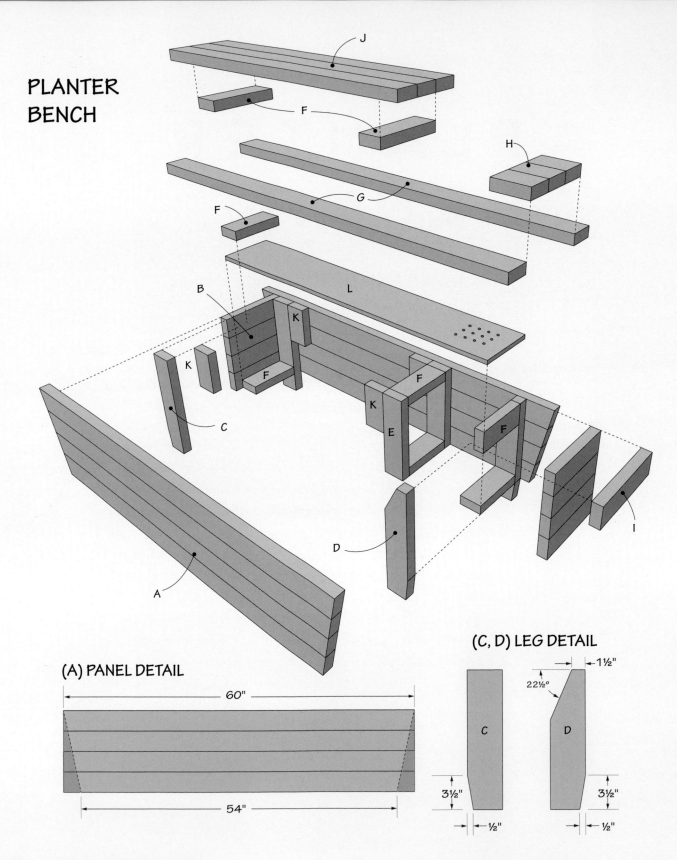

J

F

F

G

H

F

B

K

K

F

L

C

K

E

F

F

A

D

I

(A) PANEL DETAIL

60"

54"

(C, D) LEG DETAIL

1½"

22½°

C

D

3½"

3½"

½"

½"

Cutting List

Key	Qty	Description	Size
A	8	Front/Back Panels	1½ x 3½ x 60 in.
B	8	Side Panels	1½ x 3½ x 11½ in.
C	2	Storage Side Legs	1½ x 3½ x 17½ in.
D	2	Planter Side Legs	1½ x 3½ x 17½ in.
E	2	Center Framing	1½ x 3½ x 10½ in.
F	8	Crossbracing	1½ x 3½ x 9⅞ in.
G	2	Outside Seat Boards	1½ x 3½ x 62 in.
H	3	End Seat Boards	1½ x 3½ x 8¼ in.
I	1	End Seat Board Bracing	1½ x 3½ x 63 in.
J	3	Removable Seat Boards	1½ x 3½ x 42 in.
K	4	Center Seat Guides	1½ x 3½ x 7 in.
L	1	Storage Panel/Planter Bottom	¾ x 11½ x 47½ in.

Materials List

Qty	Description
12	2 x 4 in. x 8 ft. cedar
1	2 x 4 ft. x ¾ in. plywood
	2½-in. stainless-steel pocket screws
	1½-inch deck screws
	2½-inch deck screws
	Exterior glue

Tools	
Pocket hole jig	Saw
Drill/driver	Clamps
Tape measure	

How to Build a Planter Bench

(**#1**) Clamp and assemble the panels from four 2 x 4s cut to 60 inches. You can use the legs and glue to hold the panels together, but 2½-inch pocket screws every 10 inches will pull the boards together, making the panels stronger. Use a quality exterior-rated glue between the boards. Measure and mark the angles (see illustration), then, using a straightedge as a guide, cut the angles with a circular saw.

(**#2**) Trim the four legs to match the panels with a handsaw, according to the Leg Detail on page 20.

(#3) Assemble the framing/legs with 2½-inch deck screws. Notice the angled cuts in the top of the planter legs. Trimming off this waste will reduce their visibility in the planter opening. Also note the pocket holes in the crossbracing. This is to keep the top-fixed seating securely fastened.

(#4) Measure, square up, then fasten the legs/framing assembly to front/back panels.

(#5) Lay the top seating boards that will become the three parts of the seating assembly onto the assembled planter base. Center from front to back and from side to side, using small shims such as toothpicks between the boards for spacing. Clamp the outside seat boards to the base.

(#6) Drive pocket screws through the insides of the side panels and into the outer seat boards.

(#7) Also drive 2½-inch screws diagonally through the sides of the outer seat boards and into the panels.

(#8) Attach four center seat guides onto the panels. These guides will keep the center seat section in place while allowing removal. Check the fitting of the removable seat boards and adjust as necessary.

(#9) Set the center seat boards in place, shim between them with a thin spacer (toothpick), and then attach crossbracing at each end to clear the framing that supports the seat boards. Insert the storage/planter bottom panel and drive 1½-inch screws into the bottom crossbraces.

(#10) Cut three fixed-end seat boards, then apply glue and drive pocket screws up through pocket holes in the crossbracing to secure them. An additional piece of framing screwed to the outside of the side panel will help keep the fixed seat board ends stable and secure.

VERTICAL GARDEN

Grow five times as much in one small space: garden up!

Vertical gardens are new and increasingly popular among gardeners who face space limitations. Their small, efficient footprints, ease of access, and interesting appearance make them an attractive alternative to traditional gardens or planters. Many are designed to be hung from either walls or ceilings. This freestanding design allows more choices in determining its location.

The planting containers themselves are standard D-profile vinyl gutters with caps on each end. Two wood rails that stretch between two wide standards support the containers. The rails are angled to support the gutters in front and back, while the bottom is open, allowing for drainage holes.

This project can easily be built using recycled materials. It can be customized in length and height and in materials. The gutters used here allow for about four inches of soil depth, which works well for smaller plants and flowers. As an edible garden, it's perfect, as rows can be shifted up or down depending on lighting needs. In addition, as the gutters drain, they do so into the next gutter below, saving water and reducing mess. If edibles are planted, the gutters should be lined with a food-safe plastic barrier.

Consider using ⁵⁄₄ deck boards for lumber—the thicker wood will hold better and is less likely to split when screws are driven. Be sure to test-fit the rails to the gutters, as not all are built with the same profile. You can use metal gutters, like aluminum or even copper, to give the vertical garden a more dramatic look.

VERTICAL GARDEN

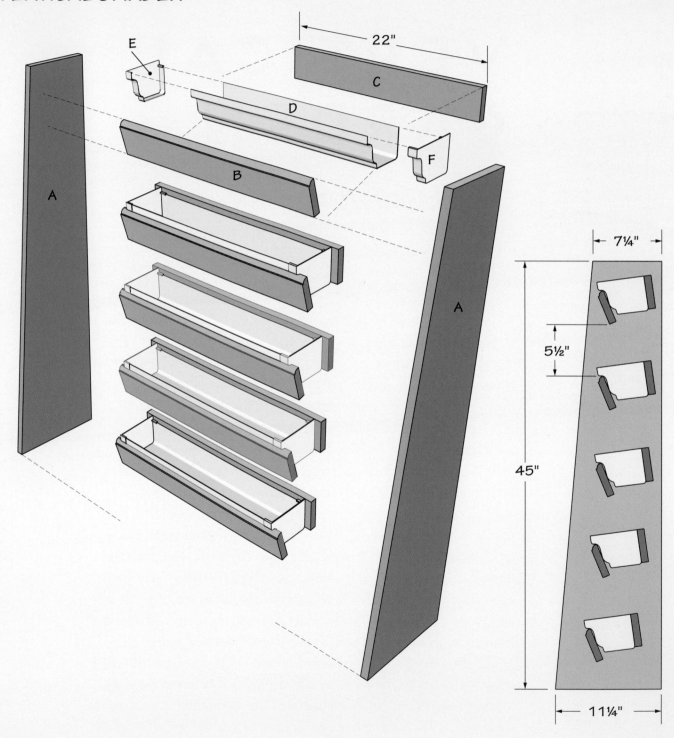

E

22"

C

D

F

B

A

A

A

7¼"

5½"

45"

11¼"

Cutting List

Key	Qty	Description	Size
A	2	Standards	¾ x 7¼ x 11¼ in.
B	5	Front Rails	¾ x 3½ x 22 in.
C	5	Back Rails	¾ x 3½ x 22 in.
D	5	Gutters	4 x 5 x 21¼ in.
E	5	Left End Caps	¾ x 4 x 5 in.
F	5	Right End Caps	¾ x 4 x 5 in.

Materials List

Qty	Description
1	1 x 12 in. x 8 ft. cedar
3	1 x 4 in. x 8 ft. cedar
1	10-ft. section vinyl gutter
5	Vinyl gutter end caps, right
5	Vinyl gutter end caps, left
	1¼-in. stainless-steel pocket screws
	2½-in. deck screws
	Adhesive caulk
	Masking tape

Tools
Aviation snips or heavy-duty scissors
Pocket hole jig
Drill/driver
¼-in. drill bit
Tape measure
Straightedge
Square
Saw
Clamps
Router (optional)
½-in. roundover bit (optional)

Two Terrific Recipes for Making Soil for Your Vertical Wall

Homemade Soil Recipes

Several homemade soil mix combinations are compatible with living wall gardens. If you're using potting soil, choose an organic product brand that includes worm castings as part of the ingredient list. If you cannot find an organic soil with worm castings, add a cup or two of worm castings directly to your soil mix if you are able; it is a great way to retain moisture. Each of these recipes can be mixed in a large bucket or wheelbarrow.

Easiest Standard Living Wall Soil Mix

- 1 part organic potting soil with worm castings
- 1 part organic rotted composted manure or plain compost
- 1 part course builder's sand

Homemade Standard Living Wall Soil Mix

- 2 parts compost
- 1 part presoaked coir peat
- 1 part vermiculite
- 1 to 2 cups worm castings

Text and photo © Shawna Coronado

Adding the best soil mix to the living wall system will help the roots of the plants adapt and grow more readily, building a successful foundation for your plants.

How to Build a Vertical Garden

(#1) Start with one 10-foot section of D-profile vinyl gutter, which can be purchased at most hardware stores and building centers. Cut the sections at 21¼ inches long using an aviation snips, a hacksaw, or even sharp scissors.

(#2) Tape the end caps, one right and one left, to the gutter lengths, then use a waterproof, white adhesive caulk to bond and seal the ends on the inner joints to keep them from slipping off and leaking water. Allow the caulk to dry.

(#3) Drill ¼-inch drainage holes along the front bottom edges of the gutters, spaced at intervals of 4 to 6 inches.

(#4) Cut two 1 x 12 boards to length to make the standards. Be wary of knotholes and any other defects as you plan your cuts.

5

6

7

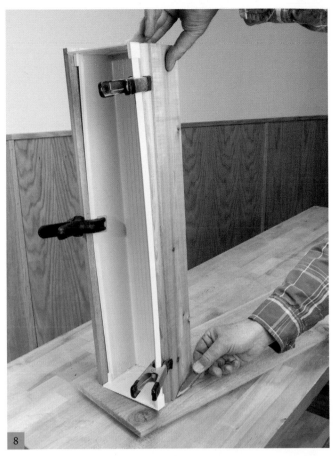

8

(#5) Using a straightedge as a guide, rip the 1 x 12 boards at an angle to create the tapered sides, leaving a minimum of 7 inches of wood at the top.

(#6) To add some detail, use a router with a ½-inch roundover bit to cut decorative profiles on the front edges of the standards. You can repeat this same detail on the lengths of 1 x 4s that will become the front support rails. If you're not comfortable using a router, you can simply break the edges with a wood rasp or file to give them a slight roundover.

(#7) Cut the front and back support rails to 22 inches. It is important that your workpieces are consistent in length. Double-check your measurements before cutting.

(#8) Using small spring clamps or tape, attach the rails to the gutters. Use the clamped gutter and rails as a template and mark the locations for each of the five gutters on one of the sides, keeping them at least 5½ inches apart.

(#9) Drill two pocket holes on the inside of each end of the front and back rails (B and C). The pocket screws will hold the frame together with no visible fasteners. If you don't want to use pocket screws (see page 15), you can attach the shelves by driving pairs of 2½-inch deck screws through counterbored pilot holes in the standards and into the ends of the shelf boards.

(#10) Following the layout marks, position and attach the back rails to the standards using 1¼-inch pocket screws.

(#11) Use one or more clamps to hold the other standard to the rails. Check for level and measure for accurate spacing, then drive screws to secure the rails to the other standard.

(#12) Test-fit a gutter section onto the rail supports to check for proper spacing and fit, making adjustments where necessary.

(#13) Line the gutter sections with a food-safe plastic, then fill with a quality potting soil mix (see page 27). Insert a small screwdriver or stick up through the gutter drainage holes to pierce the plastic liner. Plant your plants of choice.

(#14) Site your vertical garden in an area that receives at least six, and preferably eight, hours of direct sunlight per day. If it is exposed to high winds (or rambunctious kids or dogs), it's a good idea to latch the vertical garden to a deck rail or another object to keep it from blowing over.

ROLLING PLANTER WITH STORAGE

An elegant planter that rolls: fill it with veggies, container plants, or even your favorite cold beverages

A raised planter is an excellent way to create a garden with a compact and easy-access footprint. It can provide all the benefits of a typical container garden while keeping the plants at a comfortable height. No bending or reaching is required, making it easier and more enjoyable to care for garden plants. This rolling raised planter design makes a great addition to any deck, patio, or balcony.

While its clean lines and solid construction may be its best feature, it's deceptively easy to build. The 10-inch-deep planting area allows for bigger plants like tomatoes and even some root crops. It can hold containers of plants, or be lined with plastic and filled directly with soil. Or fill the planter box with ice to make a beautiful, sturdy beverage cart. A shelf adds storage and casters give it mobility, allowing the planter to be moved to maximize sun exposure (or your thirstiest guest).

RAISED PLANTER

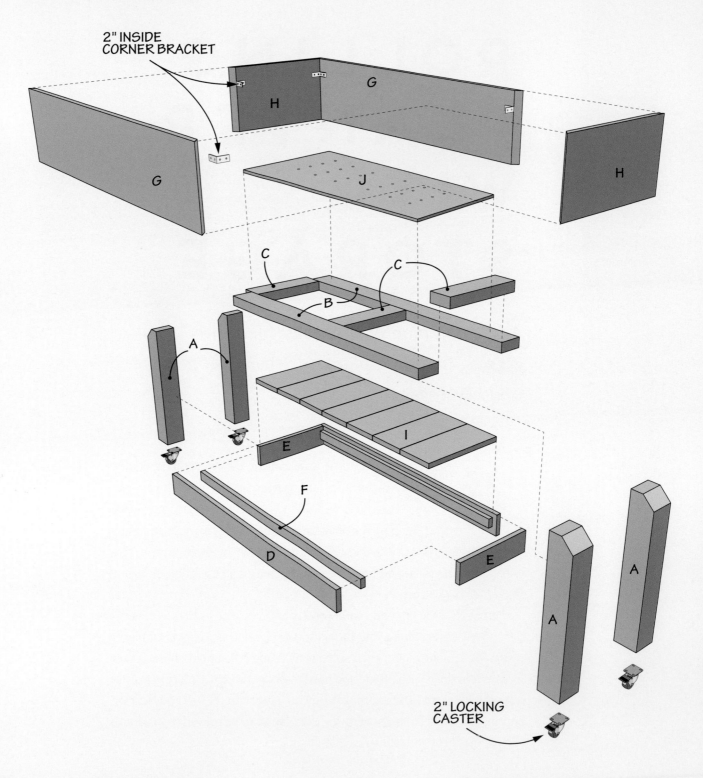

2" INSIDE
CORNER BRACKET

H

G

G

J

H

C

C

B

A

E

I

A

F

D

E

A

A

2" LOCKING
CASTER

Cutting List

Key	Qty	Description	Size
A	4	Legs	3½ x 3½ x 23 in.
B	2	Front/Back Crossbraces	1½ x 3½ x 42 in.
C	3	Side Crossbraces	1½ x 3½ x 11¾ in.
D	2	Front/Back Shelf Frames	¾ x 3½ x 42 in.
E	2	Side Shelf Frame	¾ x 3½ x 12½ in.
F	2	Shelf Cleats	¾ x 1½ x 40¼ in.
G	2	Front/Back Panels	¾ x 11/4 x 42 in.
H	2	Side Panels	¾ x 11¼ x 17 in.
I	7	Shelf Slats	¾ x 5½ x 12½ in.
J	1	Bottom Panel	¾ x 15 x 40 in.

Materials List

Qty	Description
	(Cedar or pine)
1	4 x 4 in. x 8 ft.
1	2 x 4 in. x 10 ft.
1	1 x 10 in. x 10 ft.
1	1 x 6 in. x 8 ft.
1	1 x 4 in. x 10 ft.
1	1 x 2 in. x 8 ft.
1	24 x 48 in. ¾-in. exterior plywood
	1¼-in. deck screws
	1½-in. deck screws
	2-in. deck screws
	2½-in. deck screws
	⅝-in. exterior screws
	1¼-in. pocket screws
	2-in. galvanized corner brackets
4	2-in. swivel casters
	6-mil plastic

Tools	
Drill/driver	Tape measure
Pocket hole jig	Circular saw
½-in. drill bit	Straightedge
Square	Clamps

▶ How to Build a Rolling Planter with Storage

(**#1**) Cut the legs from 4 x 4 stock, cutting 30-degree angles on one end. If you have a power miter saw, this is a snap. But it's also very easy to do with a handsaw. For the legs on the project as shown, we used relatively dark cedar post stock, which gives a nice contrast to the lighter, flat-sawn cedar 1 x 12s we used for the box sides.

(**#2**) Cut the crossbraces to length. Using a pocket hole jig, drill holes on the ends of the front, back, and side crossbraces. Drill outer and inner pairs of pocket holes on the two outer side crossbraces.

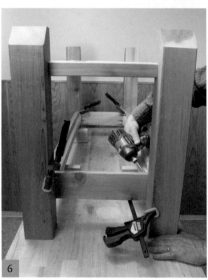

(#3) Attach the front and back crossbraces to the side crossbraces with pocket screws. Note the two pairs of pocket holes and the off-set alignment of the outer side crossbraces.

(#4) Cut the shelf frames and shelf cleats. Assemble the frames into a box using 1¼-inch pocket screws (or you can use 2½-inch deck screws driven through the overlapping frame member and into the end of the adjoining board). Attach the shelf cleats to the long box frame members so their tops are recessed ¾ inch from the top of the frame.

(#5) Use 3½-inch scraps to support the crossbracing, and then drive 2½-inch deck screws to attach the crossbraces to the legs.

(#6) Turn the assembly over and repeat the process, this time using clamps to secure the shelf frame members to the legs.

(#7) Set your circular saw to a 45-degree cutting angle and, with a straightedge, make the mitered end cuts on the 1 x 12 box panels (take care to make sure the box panels are the correct length). You could also use a jigsaw set at a 45-degree angle to make these cuts.

(#8) Drill pilot holes in the bottoms of the panels for attaching them to the crossbrace assembly.

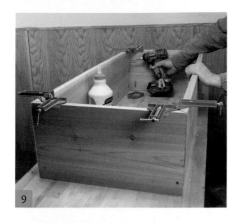

(#9) Glue and clamp the box panels to assemble the box. Drive 1½-inch deck screws through the side panels at the bottom of each of the four corners. Install 1½ x 1½-inch L-brackets at each inside corner, placed between 2 and 3 inches down from the top, to reinforce the joints. Attach them with ⅝-inch exterior-rated screws.

(#10) Place the planter box assembly between the legs and on top of the crossbracing assembly. Use a mallet and wood scrap to seat the panels against the crossbracing.

(#11) Drive 1½-inch pocket screws to attach the box panels to the crossbracing.

(#12) Use 2-inch deck screws to attach the shelf slats to the shelf cleats, being careful not to drive the screws too far and through the top surface of the shelves.

(#13) Attach 2-inch swivel casters to the bottoms of the legs.

(#14) Cut the bottom panel from a sheet of ¾-inch plywood and drill ½-inch drainage holes every 4 inches. Line the box with plastic and fill with potting soil. Poke holes into the plastic through the drainage holes for drainage. You can also use containers set directly inside the planter instead of filling the cavity with dirt.

PATIO ARMOIRE

Add 36 cubic feet of gorgeous, lockable storage capacity to any deck or patio

When you need a little extra storage space but don't want to build or buy a standard backyard shed, this outdoor locker/armoire is the solution. It can be built just about anywhere, but looks best when tucked against a fence, deck rail, or an exterior wall. The cedar-shake siding and saddle-jointed rafters give this project a classy appearance, while the metal roof lends a retro-chic look that is also easy to install.

It may look a bit complicated, but do not be fooled; it is easy to build and can be completed in a weekend. It's a good idea to have a helper when it comes to putting up the walls, but a set of long clamps will allow you to build it alone.

Materials can be swapped out to suit your individual taste or needs. The siding is nailed to ½-inch cedar pickets that act as sheathing underneath, which are in turn attached to the framing. You can use exterior-rated plywood, but the pickets are lighter and easier to haul and install. They're also inexpensive, which helps keep material costs down.

For the roof, look for recycled corrugated metal in your area; the metal used here was recycled and found online. You can use other materials for the roofing if you prefer, such as leftover cedar shakes. The footprint can be made larger or smaller as you please, but it will affect cost and time—if you do change dimensions, be careful in calculating additional material needs.

PATIO ARMOIRE

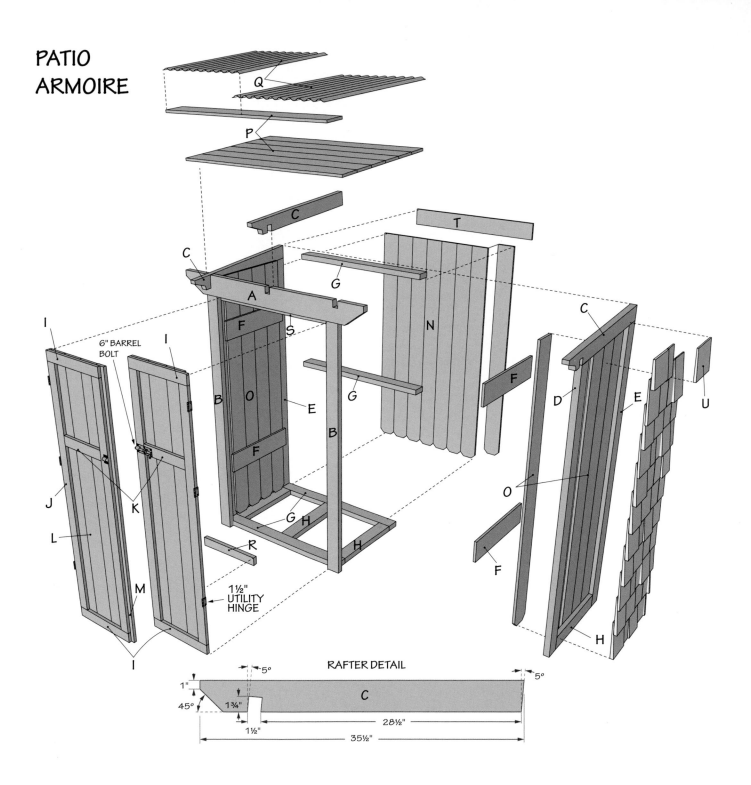

Q

P

C

C

A

F

S

I

6" BARREL BOLT

I

B

O

E

G

G

B

N

F

C

D

O

E

U

J

K

L

F

M

G H

H

R

H

1½" UTILITY HINGE

I

RAFTER DETAIL

5°

1"

45°

1¾"

C

5°

28½"

1½"

35½"

Cutting List

Key	Qty	Description	Size
A	1	Header	1½ x 5½ x 60 in.
B	2	Side Posts	1½ x 3½ x 69 in.
C	3	Rafters	1½ x 3½ x 35½ in.
D	2	Side Frame Fronts	1½ x 3½ x 71½ in.
E	2	Side Frame Rears	1½ x 3½ x 73½ in.
F	4	Side Wall Battens	½ x 5½ x 24 in.
G	4	Base/Rear Wall Framing	1½ x 3½ x 40 in.
H	5	Base/Side Wall Framing	1½ x 3½ x 21¾ in.
I	4	Top/Bottom Door Rails	¾ x 2½ x 17¾ in.
J	4	Door Stiles	¾ x 2½ x 62 in.
K	2	Cross-Rails	¾ x 2½ x 12⅞ in.
L	6	Door Panels	½ x 5½ x 68½ in.
M	1	Astragal	¾ x 1½ x 68 in.
N	8	Rear Sheathing Boards	½ x 5½ x 72 in.
O	8	Side Sheathing Boards	½ x 5½ x 72 in.
P	7	Roof Sheathing Boards	½ x 5½ x 48 in.
Q	2	Metal Roofing (optional)	¼ x 26 x 39 in.
R	6	Door Panel Battens	¾ x 1½ x 15 in.
S	1	Door Stop	¾ x 1½ x 38 in.
T	1	Rear Sheathing Top	½ x 5½ x 44 in.
U	1	Cedar Shake Bundle	18 in.

Materials List

Qty	Description
	(Cedar)
1	2 x 6 in. x 8 ft.
13	2 x 4 in. x 8 ft.
29	1 x 6 in. x 6 ft. pickets
4	1 x 4 in. x 8 ft.
3	1 x 2 in. x 8 ft.
	18-in. cedar shingles (1 bundle)
1	1 x 26 in. x 8 ft. corrugated metal roofing
	1½-in. deck screws
	2½-in. deck screws
	1¼-in. pocket screws
	1-in. ring-shank blunt-tip nails
	1½-in. hex washer head roofing screws
6	1½-in. utility hinges
	6-in. barrel bolt
	6-mil plastic

Tools	
Drill/driver	Straightedge
Pocket hole jig	Square
½-in. drill bit	Level
Tape measure	Clamps
Circular saw	

How to Build a Patio Armoire

(#1) Cut the cedar to length for the base and back framing, rafters, front, back, and sides. Trim off the corners on these parts with a handsaw (see Rafter Detail, page 40). Cut notches in the top front and rafters to create saddle joints, according to the same diagram. Use a handsaw to cut the shoulders of the notches and then finish removing the waste wood with a sharp wood chisel.

(#2) Assemble the base frame that the armoire sits upon, and then assemble the frames for the sides, using 2½-inch exterior-rated screws to form pocket screw joints.

(#3) Assemble the front frame by joining the top to the side frame members. Wherever possible, screw from the inside of the framing.

(#4) Screw the base frame to the side frames to make pocket screw joints (you don't have to use pocket screws, but they are fast to make and strong compared to other methods of using mechanical fasteners (such as toe-screwing) to join the boards. Check for level and plumb as you work.

(#5) Attach a pair of 2 x 4s on the flat between the side frames to create the back wall, and complete the structural framing of the carcase.

(#6) Begin installing the three rafters by placing them on top of the framed carcase with the front ends seated in the saddle notches. Attach them to the front and rear top plates. Clamp the parts together to hold them exactly in position as you fasten them to the header and wall framing.

Shake that Thing

Shakes are a classic and beautiful covering for homes and sheds. They add a charm and rustic finish that only gets better over time. My brother-in-law, a professional carpenter, once commented that cedar shakes "never leak." This is true because cedar shakes will expand when wet, and as they expand they close any gaps that may be present between the boards. A shed I built over 10 years ago using hand-split cedar shake siding has never leaked, even in wind-driven rains during the most violent storms. Shakes also come in other materials, such as cement board, vinyl, and fiberglass.

Installing shakes is relatively easy. Begin with a starter course, which is covered by a second layer. Leave a ⅛-inch space between each shake, attaching them with two ring-shank blunt-tip nails with a minimum 7/32-inch head. Make sure that the joints are not aligned over subsequent courses. Leave a space between the gaps of at least 1½ inches from the shingles in the previous course. Ideally, no joints should be aligned over three subsequent courses. Do not allow a gap to occur over a knot. A good rule of thumb for walls is to expose between 5 and 6 inches of the shake between rows.

Install subsequent courses on the rest of the wall according to the chosen exposure. Keep the courses straight and level. To make shingle alignment easier, tack a furring strip beneath the exposure line or make a chalk line. A utility knife can be used to score and snap shakes to size. For small wall sections like this project, a small level works well.

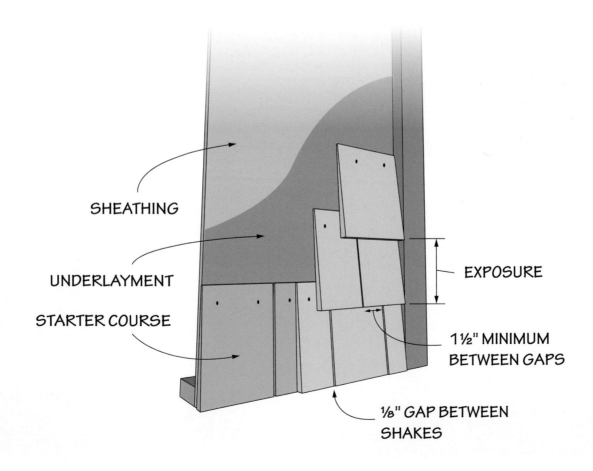

SHEATHING

UNDERLAYMENT

STARTER COURSE

EXPOSURE

1½" MINIMUM
BETWEEN GAPS

⅛" GAP BETWEEN
SHAKES

7

8

(**#7**) Use cedar fence pickets as sheathing, attaching them on the outside for the back wall, and on the inside for the sidewalls. The top rear of the side sheathing may need to be notched to allow for the rear top plate.

(**#8**) Also attach cedar fence pickets to the tops of the rafters to create sheathing for the roof.

(**#9**) To help secure the sheathing to the structure, screw battens cut from the cedar pickets onto the interior wall. Overlap them slightly at the ends and secure to the framing.

(**#10**) Attach the shakes, starting from the bottom. They can be lined up or staggered. Use ring-shank blunt-tip nails to attach them to the sheathing. Use two nails per shake and nail in the area that will be covered by the next row of shakes. (See Shake that Thing on the previous page.)

9

10

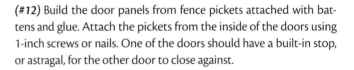

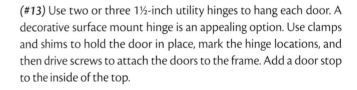

(**#11**) Build the doors using 1 x 3 and 1 x 4 cedar. Cut the top, center, and bottom rails, then drill pocket holes for screwing the rails to the stiles.

(**#12**) Build the door panels from fence pickets attached with battens and glue. Attach the pickets from the inside of the doors using 1-inch screws or nails. One of the doors should have a built-in stop, or astragal, for the other door to close against.

(**#13**) Use two or three 1½-inch utility hinges to hang each door. A decorative surface mount hinge is an appealing option. Use clamps and shims to hold the door in place, mark the hinge locations, and then drive screws to attach the doors to the frame. Add a door stop to the inside of the top.

(**#14**) Install the roof covering. You can use the remainder of the shakes to match the walls, or install corrugated metal (or fiberglass) roof panels, as is being shown here. Add a barrel bolt or, if you want to be able to lock the armoire, install a hasp that will accept a padlock. You can apply an exterior finish with UV-protection if you want the armoire to remain cedar toned, or you can simply let it weather to a natural gray color.

6

DROP-DOWN WALL CABINET

Store unsightly supplies in this unobtrusive wall cabinet with a convenient drop-down work surface

Outdoor kitchens are all the rage now, but preparing for outdoors can be aggravating because it usually means going back and forth multiple times to the kitchen, pantry, or garage. And most of the time, you realize you forgot something just as the steaks are nearing perfection but the grill is starting to flare up. Wouldn't it be nice to have a small storage area for your grilling supplies (or anything else you want to store) that would be easy to access while keeping items out of the weather?

If you answer yes to this question, this project is for you. In addition to your grilling tools, a drop-down outdoor cabinet is the perfect place for suntan lotions, bug repellent, cleaning supplies, or a first-aid kit. It can also act as a place for beverages and food, or a place to stage your music while entertaining. The drop-down cabinet shown here hangs on the wall and has a drop-down door that is hinged on the bottom and is supported by chains so it can double as a work surface when the cabinet is open.

Use lumber that suits the environment where it will hang, and build it as bug and critter tight as you can. Consider adding a lock to keep children safe. You can add custom touches like hardware, lighting, or ephemera that will personalize the cabinet.

WALL CABINET

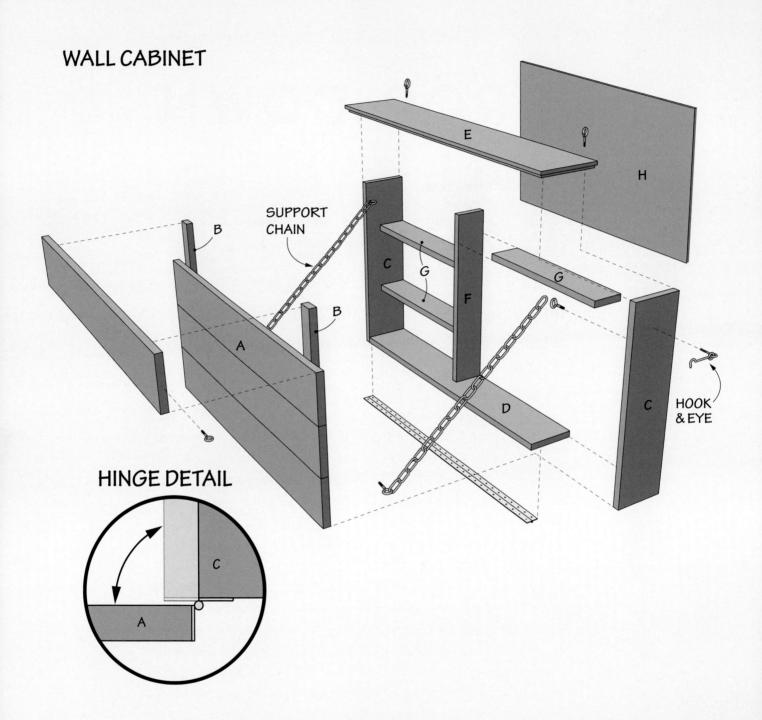

SUPPORT
CHAIN

B

B

A

E

H

C

G

G

F

D

C

HOOK
& EYE

HINGE DETAIL

C

A

Cutting List

Key	Qty	Description	Size
A	4	Door Panels	¾ x 5½ x 36 in.
B	2	Door Battens	¾ x 1½ x 20 in.
C	2	Cabinet Sides	¾ x 5½ x 22 in.
D	1	Cabinet Bottom	¾ x 5½ x 34¼ in.
E	1	Cabinet Top	¾ x 7¼ x 38 in.
F	1	Divider	¾ x 5½ x 21¼ in.
G	3	Shelves	¾ x 3½ x 16-78 in.
H	1	Back Panel	¼ x 35¾ x 22½ in.

Materials List

Qty	Description
	(Cedar)
1	1 x 8 in. x 4 ft.
3	1 x 6 in. x 8 ft.
1	1 x 4 in. x 8 ft.
3	1 x 2 in. x 8 ft.
1	24 x 48 in. ¼-in. plywood
1	30-in. piano hinge
	60-in. chain
6	Eye hooks
2	Hook-and-eye latches
	1½-in. stainless-steel screws
	1¼-in. pocket screws

Tools	
Drill/driver	Circular saw
Pocket hole jig	Straightedge
Tape measure	Level
Square	Clamps

How to Build a Drop-Down Wall Cabinet

(#1) Cut the bottom and side frame members for the cabinet box from 1 x 6 stock (we used rough cedar). Cut the top frame member to length from 1 x 8 stock. If you have a router, you can add a decorative edge, or cut a 45-degree bevel with a circular saw or hand plane to the profile of the front edges of the box.

(#2) Using a pocket hole jig, drill pocket holes in the bottom box frame member where it will join with the shelves.

(#3) Glue and clamp the cabinet box together, then check to make sure it is square. Drill countersunk pilot holes in the top, then use 1½-inch brass or stainless-steel screws to fasten the top to the sides.

(#4) Measure and cut the interior divider and shelves to length from 1 x 4 stock. Use pocket hole screws to attach them to the inside of the cabinet.

(#5) Build the drop-down door from more 1 x 6 stock, using a combination of pocket hole screws, glue, and two 1 x 2 battens. The battens are 2 inches shorter than the overall height of the door. Space them 1½ inches from the bottom.

(#6) Test-fit the door to the cabinet, then attach a brass piano hinge (brass is a good exterior metal) to the bottom of the cabinet and the door. A thin strip of weather stripping can be applied to the door for a better seal.

(#7) The cabinet doesn't require a back panel, but installing one is a good idea if you want to keep out rain, dirt, and pests. Use an exterior-rated plywood to make the back panel. Cut, glue, and clamp the panel, then attach it to the back of the cabinet box with 1¼-inch screws.

(#8) Screw brass eyehooks to the inside of the cabinet sides and to the faces of the battens to secure the door support chains. Add a hook-and-eye latch (inset photo) to each side of the cabinet to hold the door closed. Mount the cabinet using metal eyehooks screwed into the top. Then hang the cabinet on 1½-inch screws driven securely into the house siding, preferably at wall-framing member locations. Apply a finish as desired.

ARBOR BENCH

Create a romantic getaway right on your deck or patio with this impressive arbor and bench combo

Garden benches can take on an almost unlimited number of forms, but when you combine a comfortable, roomy bench with an overhead arbor, you've got a structure that will be a destination for any outdoor living. And when you place your arbor bench in the perfect spot, it becomes a mini getaway that offers the promise of sanctuary. If you build one, you'll have a furnishing that is not only beautiful, but is a great place to read, have a conversation, or just sit and reflect.

This easy design allows construction in a day. Be sure to place the arbor out of windy areas, and if wind is an issue, be sure to use footings or post anchors to keep the structure stable. A finish of spar urethane or any other exterior finish with UV protection will help protect the wood and keep it looking fresh, making your arbor bench an enjoyable retreat for many years.

ARBOR BENCH

CROSSBRACE DETAIL

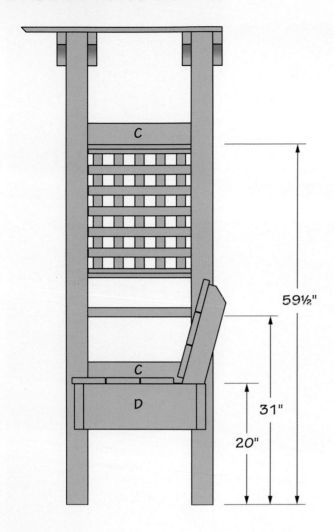

59½"

31"

20"

C

C

D

Cutting List

Key	Qty	Description	Size
A	4	Beams	¾ x 5½ x 60 in.
B	4	Posts	3½ x 3½ x 78 in.
C	4	Post Crossbraces	3½ x 3½ x 17 in.
D	3	Seat Framing Sides	1½ x 5½ x 18½ in.
E	2	Seat Framing Front/Back	1½ x 5½ x 41½ in.
F	2	Seat Back Supports	1½ x 3½ x 17 in.
G	6	Seat Boards	1 x 5½ x 41½ in.
H	2	Armrests	1½ x 3½ x 17 in.
I	4	Lattice Retainers	¾ x 1½ x 17 in.
J	2	Lattice Panels	1 x 17 x 22 in.
K	9	Purlins	¾ x 1½ x 28 in.

Materials List

Qty	Description
	(Cedar)
4	4 x 4 in. x 8 ft.
5	2 x 6 in. x 8 ft.
1	2 x 4 in. x 8 ft.
4	1 x 2 in. x 8 ft.
3	⁵⁄₄ x 6 in. x 8 ft. decking
1	24 x 48 lattice panel
	6-in. timber lag screws
	2½-in. deck screws
	1½-in. stainless-steel trim head screws

Tools	
Drill/driver	Straightedge
Tape measure	Level
Square	Clamps
Circular saw	File or rasp
Compass	Jigsaw

How to Build an Arbor Bench

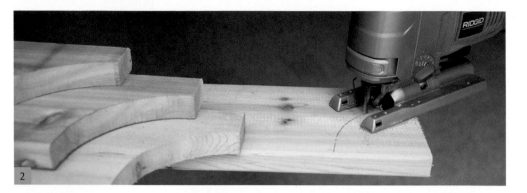

(#1) The top of the arbor is created by sandwiching pairs of 1 x 6 around the tops of the front and back posts. The beam members are profiled on the ends for visual appeal. Start by cutting the beam members to length from 1 x 6 stock (we used cedar). Then use a compass to lay out a 3½-inch-radius cutting line on the bottom corner of each beam member.

(#2) Make the profile cuts on the beam members' ends with a jigsaw. Smooth out the profile cuts with a file or rasp.

(#3) Cut the 4 x 4 posts and crossbraces to length and then clamp them together, as shown in the Crossbrace Detail on page 55. Lay the clamped assembly on a flat, level surface and fasten the parts together by driving 6-inch timber screws through the posts and into the crossbraces. Drive at least two (three is better) at each joint. Most timber screws are self-tapping, but if they give you any difficulty, drill pilot holes.

(#4) Cut the four members of the seat frame box to length and then assemble the seat frame by driving 2½-inch stainless-steel or coated deck screws, three per joint.

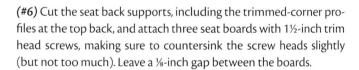

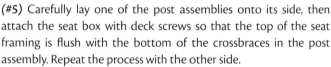

(#5) Carefully lay one of the post assemblies onto its side, then attach the seat box with deck screws so that the top of the seat framing is flush with the bottom of the crossbraces in the post assembly. Repeat the process with the other side.

(#6) Cut the seat back supports, including the trimmed-corner profiles at the top back, and attach three seat boards with 1½-inch trim head screws, making sure to countersink the screw heads slightly (but not too much). Leave a ⅛-inch gap between the boards.

(#7) Attach the seat back supports to the posts with three or four screws driven at each post. The back corner of supports should sit at the center of the back seat framing, and the top seat board should be at or near the center of the posts.

(#8) Using 1½-inch trim head screws, attach the seat boards to the top edges of the seat framing box, countersinking the screw heads. Space the screws carefully so you have a regular pattern with well-aligned screw heads—they will be visible and a sloppy pattern will make the project look a bit amateurish.

9

10

11

12

(#9) Attach the decorative beam members to the tops of the posts with trim head screws. The tops of the beam members should be flush with the tops of the posts, with equal overhangs on all posts.

(#10) Cut the armrests to length and fasten them securely between the front and back post pairs. Pocket screws driven into pocket holes on the bottoms of the armrests make a strong joint, or you can cut blocking and attach it to the posts below the armrests to support them.

(#11) Add visual privacy and wind blocking by installing cedar lattice panels in the sides of the post assemblies. Cut the lattice (a prefabricated product) to fit. Cut and install 1 x 2 lattice retainer strips, and then attach the lattice panels to the retainer strips with short screws.

(#12) Cut the decorative purlins to length to fit on top of the structure, making it truly an arbor. Miter cut the front ends of each purlin at about 30 degrees and fasten them to the beam pairs spaced at 5½-inch intervals (a 1 x 6 makes a good spacer to assure even spacing). Start with the center purlin, working out toward the ends and using 1¼-trim head screws to fasten them. Apply a finish as desired.

OPTION: Add a Stabilizer

If your arbor bench will be located in an area that will be subject to high winds, or if you're just a little concerned about it tipping over, you can add stability to the structure by adding a pair of stabilizers to the bottom. Simply cut two pieces of 1 x 6 or 2 x 6 to about 40 inches in length and fasten them to the post bottoms parallel to the arbor bench sides. For decorative effect and to reduce the hazards of tripping, echo the profile cuts you made in the tops of the beam members (see steps 1 and 2).

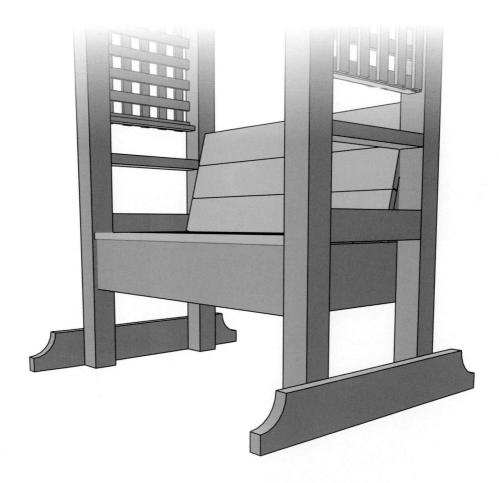

STORAGE BENCH/ DOCK BOX

Rustic charm coupled with clean, contemporary lines make this bench/box at home anywhere

Simply put, this bench is a box. A great convenience in any backyard or patio area, a storage bench does double duty, as its name implies. It provides a comfortable place to sit while also offering the capacity to hold any number of items you're likely to need outdoors, such as cushions, bag chairs, or lawn games.

Somewhat reminiscent of an antique blanket chest, this design is classically simple. It employs edge-glued 1 x 4 boards for most of its construction. Battens on the inside of the chest help hold it together, and the mitered legs give it a polished, refined appearance. Use a quality adhesive to help give the structure additional strength. Hardware can also be added to improve its overall durability.

The Storage Bench/Dock Box is built with interior-grade (non-treated) pine, so it is important that you apply a weather-resistant finish to both the exterior and the interior. The high-gloss of spar varnish makes it an excellent choice. Or consider a lightly tinted exterior stain to deepen the wood tones. And don't forget the paint option: a glossy, battleship gray always looks appropriate on dock boxes. Or choose a brighter hue to add some color to your outdoor areas.

61

STORAGE BENCH

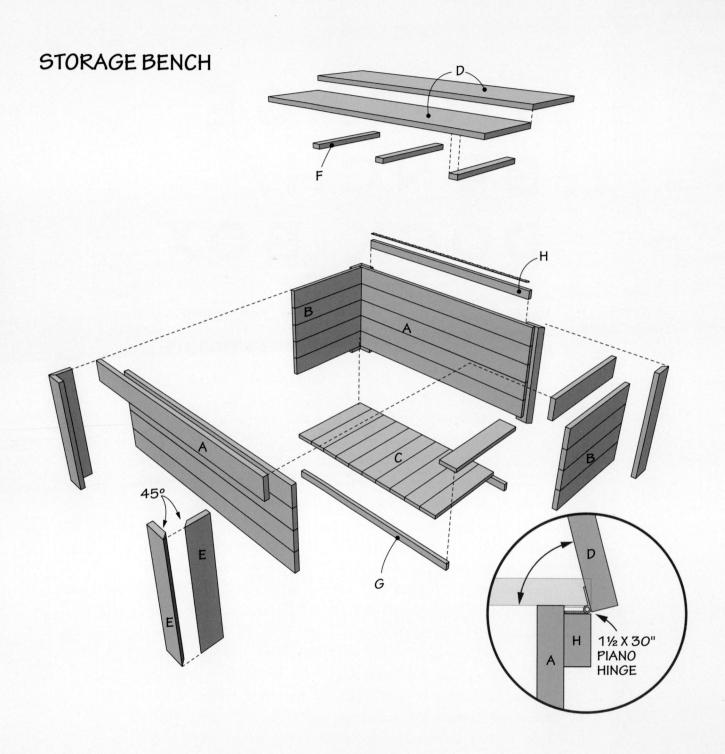

D

F

H

B

A

45°

E

E

A

C

G

B

D

A   H   1½ X 30"
PIANO
HINGE

Cutting List

Key	Qty	Description	Size
A	10	Front/Back Panels	¾ x 3½ x 40 in.
B	10	Side Panels	¾ x 3½ x 17⅓ in.
C	11	Bottom Panel	¾ x 3½ x 17½ in.
D	2	Lid Panels	¾ x 11¼ x 42 in.
E	8	Leg Pairs	¾ x 3¼ x 18¾ in.
F	3	Battens	¾ x 1½ x 14 in.
G	2	Bottom Support Strips	¾ x 1½ x 37 in.
H	1	Hinge Support Strip	¾ x 1½ x 35 in.

Materials List

Qty	Description
	(Pine)
11	1 x 4 in. x 8 ft.
2	1 x 2 in. x 8 ft.
1	30-in. piano hinge
1	1 x 12 x 8 ft.
	1¼-in. deck screws
	1¼-in. finish nails
	Exterior glue
	Wood stain or paint

Tools	
Drill/driver	Straightedge
Tape measure	Sander
Square	Clamps
Circular saw	Miter saw

▶ How to Build a Storage Bench/Dock Box

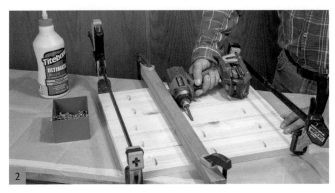

(#1) Cut the boards you'll use to create the laminated front, back, and side panels from 1 x 4 stock. Use the clearest stock you can find. Here, interior-grade No. 2 or better clear pine is used.

> **TIP:** Cut the boards for the glue-up a couple of inches over-long so you can trim the panels to length and get an even edge.

(#2) Glue and clamp the 1 x 4s together to create the glue-up panels. Use quality exterior-grade glue. It's also a good idea to clamp a wood caul or two on top of the assembly to keep the individual boards from shifting as the glue dries. If you wish, you may use pocket screws or other methods to reinforce the edge-glued joints, but in most cases a good glue joint will be plenty strong.

(#3) Trim the individual glue-up panels for the sides, front, and back to length with a straightedge guide and a circular saw. Use a fine blade to get the smoothest cut you can. You may use pocket screws to join the box panels together, or you can simply end-screw them through pilot holes, because the screw heads will be concealed by the mitered legs. Use a framing square to test the joints for square and adjust your clamp pressure as necessary to bring things into square.

(#4) Cut the 1 x 4 boards for the legs to length. You'll need eight workpieces. On the better edge of each board (if there is one), make a 45-degree bevel cut. A circular saw set at a 45-degree cutting angle will manage this as long as the workpiece is very secure and you use a straightedge guide.

> **TIP:** You may find it easier to cut the bevels on the board edges from the full-length and then cut them into leg lengths.

(#5) Pre-assemble the pairs of beveled boards into four legs by applying glue along the beveled edges of mating boards and then driving 1¼-inch finish nails through pilot holes along each beveled joint to reinforce it. A pair of 90-degree corner clamps like the ones seen above will make this job easier and you'll get virtually fool-proof results.

(#6) With the box upside-down on a flat surface, glue and clamp the legs to each corner. The legs should extend 1¼ inches past the bottom edge of the box so you will have some space beneath the box and the box will not make contact with the ground. Reinforce the joints with 1¼-inch screws driven through the inside of the box and into the legs. Use plenty, but take care not to overdrive them to the point where the screw tips break the outer leg surface.

(#7) Add a 1 x 2 support between the corner braces at the top of the assembled box for the piano hinge. Allow a space of ⅛ inch for the folded piano hinge (see illustration on page 62).

(#8) Add two more 1 x 2 cleats to the bottom of the box to support the bottom panel. Build the lid panel from two pieces of 1 x 12 stock, using the same edge-gluing technique as for the side, front, and back panels. For strength and rigidity when the project is in bench mode (that is, when someone is sitting on it), add 1 x 2 battens to the underside of the glue-up once the glue has dried.

(#9) Sand all the wood surfaces to even out the panels. Be careful not to take too much wood away, exposing the bevels, when sanding the legs.

(#10) Stain or paint the bench with an exterior-grade product (see page 61). It is also a good idea to finish the interior to protect the wood and to help minimize any bowing or warping of the wood.

(#11) Fasten the lid to the box with a brass piano hinge.

(#12) Add two brass restraint chains between the side panels and the battens to hold the lid upright.

TIMBER BENCH

A beefy undercarriage and sturdy benchtop are muted beautifully by refined Eastern-inspired styling

Having a place to sit and reflect on a deck or patio is only natural, and creating your own seating is a rewarding way to customize your space. Simpler is often better in outdoor design, and this bench is both simple and beautiful. Inspired by Japanese timber benches, it boasts contrasting wood tones that enhance its visual interest.

The bench uses posts as the basis of its supporting structure. The notching that's required to join the legs and beams is easy to accomplish with just a circular saw and chisel. Long deck screws driven to reinforce the notched joints make construction quick and sturdy and are recommended. But if you wish to be a purist about it, many of the Japanese-style benches this design is based upon are fully knock-down-able—they use no fasteners whatsoever, so they can be easily disassembled and transported. With a few design modifications, you could accomplish the same no-fastener effect with this plan.

TIMBER BENCH

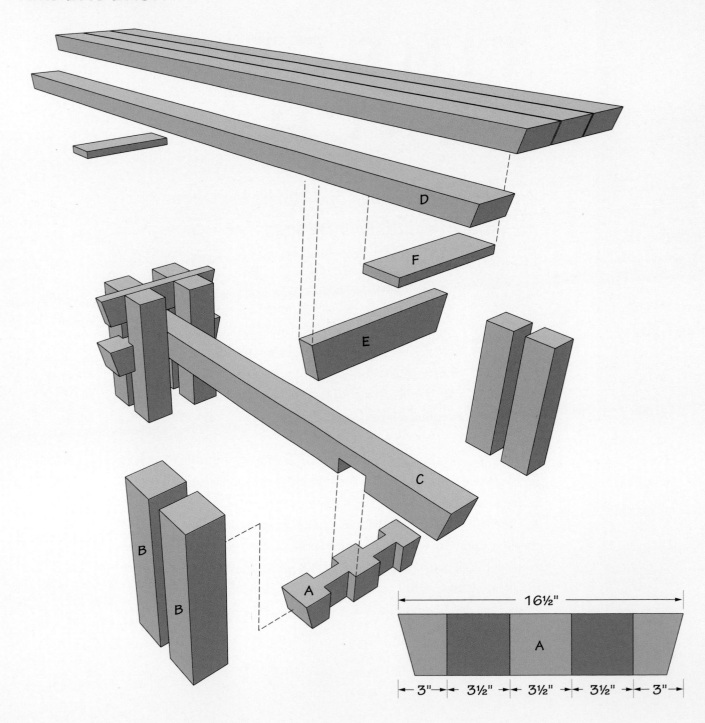

D

F

E

C

B

B

A

16½"

A

3" 3½" 3½" 3½" 3"

Cutting List

Key	Qty	Description	Size
A	2	Leg/Beam Supports	3½ x 3½ x 16½ in.
B	8	Legs	3½ x 3½ x 16 in.
C	1	Beam	3½ x 3½ x 58 in.
D	4	Seat Slats	3½ x 1½ x 62 in.
E	2	Seat Supports	1½ x 1½ x 16½ in.
F	2	Slat Spreaders	1½ x 1½ x 11 in.

Materials List

Qty	Description
	(Cedar)
3	4 x 4 in. x 8 ft.
5	2 x 4 in. x 8 ft.
1	2 x 2 in. x 4 ft.
	4-in. deck screws
	2-in. pocket screws

Tools	
Drill/driver	Chisel
Tape measure	Straightedge
Square	Level
Circular saw	Clamps
Handsaw	

▶ How to Build a Timber Bench

(**#1**) Cut the parts to length. Make sure your cuts are square and the lengths are accurate. Cut 15-degree angles on the ends of the leg/beam supports and the beam.

(**#2**) Set the cutting depth of your circular saw to 1 inch. Mark the notch locations on the leg supports.

(#3) Make multiple passes with the saw to kerf the wood and to remove the waste from the notch area. Be careful to stay within the marked areas and be sure your workpieces are well secured.

(#4) Finish removing the waste wood from the notch areas with a sharp chisel in the 1-inch range. Get the bottoms of the notches as smooth as you can with the chisel.

(#5) Sand the notches smooth with this clever shop-built sanding tool. It's simply a block of 1x stock cut to fit snugly within an 18 x 3-inch sanding belt.

(#6) Set a leg/beam support into the notched cutout on two of the legs as shown. Drive 4-inch deck screws at the joint to connect the parts.

(#7) Screw the inside legs into the leg/beam support with more 4-inch deck screws, slightly countersinking the screw heads.

(#8) Notch the beam on each end, cutting, chiseling, and sanding in the same fashion as the leg/beam supports. Lay the beam upside-down on a piece of scrap 4 x 4, then set the leg assembly on it, driving 4-inch deck screws to connect the beam to the leg/beam supports.

(#9) Drill pocket holes into the seat slat supports, spacing them so that they match up with the seat slats. Drive 2-inch pocket screws, being careful not to drive them too far so that they break the top surface of the seat slats. Use a spreader board on each end of the seat slats to keep the slats evenly spaced.

(#10) Set the seat assembly into the leg pair assemblies using a mallet, if necessary. Then drive 4-inch screws through the inside legs and into the seat slat supports. Finish as desired.

ADIRONDACK CHAIR

Extra-broad arms and a beefy seat made from 2 x 2s are two of the elements that set this Adirondack chair apart from others that bear the name

Thomas Lee would be amazed at the proliferation of furnishings based on that first Westport Plank Chair he designed in 1903. It's an American classic that has lived on. There are many variations to the original design, including double Adirondack chairs and even giant Adirondack chairs that are built commonly as novelty items. Although there are some tricky elements to the design, designing your own Adirondack chair is a relatively easy project when it comes to customizing.

This design maintains the classic look but has some upscale variations. The front legs are larger and tapered, and the back legs are streamlined and curved. The seat is made from 2 x 2 stock, and the back features a cloud lift-styled radius. Trim head screws allow for quicker assembly. Fill any nail or screw holes with stainable putty before staining and sealing.

ADIRONDACK CHAIR

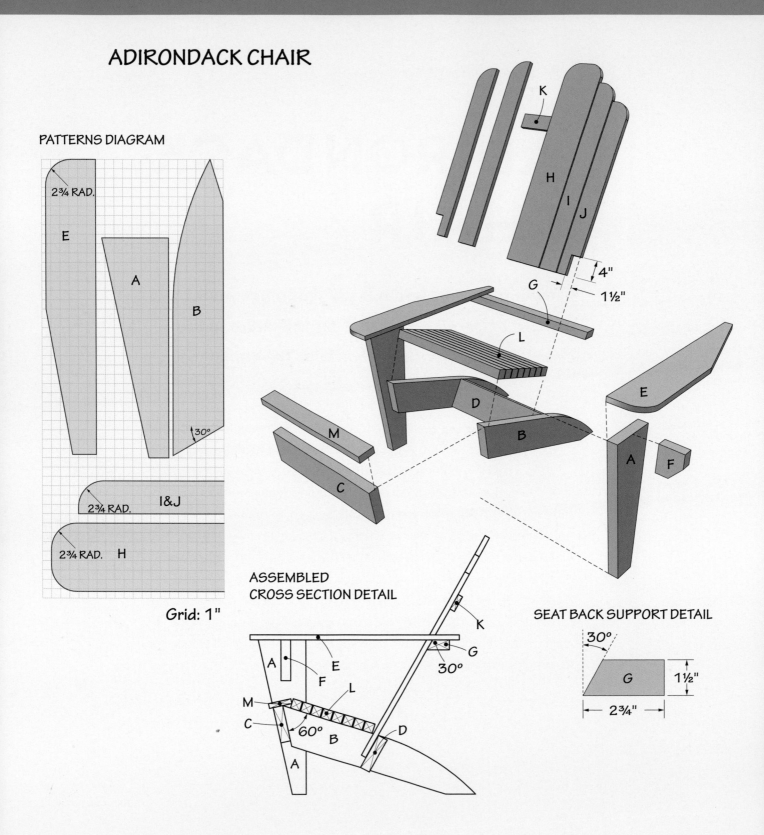

PATTERNS DIAGRAM

2¾ RAD.

E

A

B

30°

2¾ RAD.   I&J

2¾ RAD.   H

Grid: 1"

K

H
I
J

4"

1½"

G

L

M

C

D

B

E

A

F

ASSEMBLED
CROSS SECTION DETAIL

K

A   E   G

F   30°

M   L

C   60°   B   D

A

SEAT BACK SUPPORT DETAIL

30°

G   1½"

2¾"

Cutting List

Key	Qty	Description	Size
A	2	Front Legs	1½ x 7 x 23½ in.
B	2	Back Legs	1½ x 5½ x 31⅝ in.
C	1	Front Cross Support	1½ x 3½ x 22 in.
D	1	Rear Cross Support	1½ x 3½ x 19 in.
E	2	Armrests	¾ x 5½ x 32½ in.
F	2	Armrest Supports	1½ x 3½ x 6 in.
G	1	Seat Back Support	1½ x 2¾ x 27 in.
H	1	Seat Back Center Plank	¾ x 7¼ x 38 in.
I	2	Seat Back Inside Planks	¾ x 3½ x 35 in.
J	2	Seat Back Outside Planks	¾ x 3½ x 32 in.
K	1	Seat Back Batten	¾ x 1½ x 20½ in.
L	8	Seat Slats	1½ x 1½ x 22 in.
M	1	Front Seat Trim	¾ x 3½ x 22 in.

Materials List

Qty	Description
	(Cedar or pine)
1	2 x 8 in. x 4 ft.
1	2 x 6 in. x 10 ft.
1	2 x 4 in. x 8 ft.
2	2 x 2 in. x 8 ft.
1	1 x 8 in. x 4 ft.
1	1 x 6 in. x 8 ft.
2	1 x 4 in. x 8 ft.
	1¼-in. deck screws
	1½-in. trim head screws
	2½-in. trim head screws
	Teak oil or polyurethane

Tools	
Drill/driver	Straightedge
Tape measure	Level
Square	Clamps
Circular saw	Jigsaw
Belt sander	Pocket hole jig

▶ How to Build an Adirondack Chair

(#1) Cut the front legs to length. Using a straightedge and circular saw, cut a taper from the bottom to the top of each workpiece (see Patterns Diagram, previous page). Insert scrap wood under the leg to protect your work surface. Also cut tapers for the armrests. Tip your saw base to 30 degrees and cut a bevel along one edge of the seat-back support

(#2) Cut the back legs to length. Cut a 30-degree angle on the front, then bend a thin piece of wood to the profile for the legs and clamp it to the leg stock so you can trace the curve to form a cutting line.

(#3) Using a jigsaw, cut the curve into the tops of the back legs. Also cut curves into the outside front corners of the armrests.

(#4) Gang-clamp similar parts together with the straight edges aligned. Secure them and sand with a belt sander to smooth and even out the curves so they follow the diagram and they are identical on the workpieces.

(#5) Using a jigsaw, cut the curved arches into the tops of the seat back planks. On the bottoms of the outer slats, cut a 1½-by-4-inch notch as shown in the illustration on page 74).

(#6) Screw the back legs to the front cross support using 2½-inch trim head screws. Toe-screwing is acceptable, but pocket holes will be cleaner and stronger.

(#7) Drive 2½-inch trim head screws through the back legs to attach them to the front legs. Check the level and plumb of the front legs. Trim any extra wood required off the bottom of the back legs to make sure the front legs are sitting correctly. Check plumb from the rear of the front legs.

(#8) Apply glue and then drive 1½-inch stainless-steel trim head screws to attach the armrests to the front legs. Add the armrest support to the underside using 2½-inch trim head screws on the side and 1½ inch trim heads screws on the top. Attach the back to the legs, but use only one screw per side in case it needs to be slightly adjusted once the seat back is installed.

(#9) Arrange the seat back planks using screws as spacers, and then lightly clamp the assembly to hold it in place. Install a 1 x 2 batten with 1¼-inch trim head screws to hold the slats together.

(#10) Screw the seat back support to the underside of the armrests using 2½-inch trim head screws. Secure and check the angle and location of the seat back. Drive the remaining screws to secure the rear crossbrace to the back legs. Install the seat back by using clamps to hold it in place and then by screwing it to the rear crossbrace with 1½-inch screws. Check for level on the armrests, adjusting the height of the seat back on the seat back support. Finally, drive 1¼-inch trim head screws through the seat-back planks and into the seat back support.

(#11) Starting at the rear, attach the seat slats to the back legs with 2½-inch trim head screws. Attach the front seat trim to the front crossbrace with 1½-inch trim head screws. Sand and finish with a teak oil or polyurethane.

CLUB CHAIR

Classic retro lines, simple joinery, and store-bought cushions make for easy outdoor building (and living)

Few things are more comfortable than relaxing in a club chair with a good book and an ice-cold lemonade on a warm summer day. It's a perfect place to kick back. Club chairs are traditionally made with cushions, which can really make a difference in comfort, so get some additional ideas before you begin by looking at other chairs and cushions. In the end, the cushions you choose will dictate the final size of your chair (unless you happen to be a whiz with a sewing machine and can make your own cushions to fit). The standard-sized cushions used here were purchased from a department store. You can also buy stock cushions at many home center stores or order from online merchants for more choices in color and styles.

Its straightforward design makes this chair easy to construct. Mahogany is a great choice for material as it weathers well. Other good wood choices are cedar, cypress, or redwood. Use s4s (sanded four sides) boards, and if needed, have the lumberyard mill the lumber to achieve straight edges. Assembly is achieved through pocket hole joinery, with metal brackets added to the interior seat frame to add strength. Finish with teak oil and a spar urethane to highlight the rich mahogany color and grain.

CLUB CHAIR

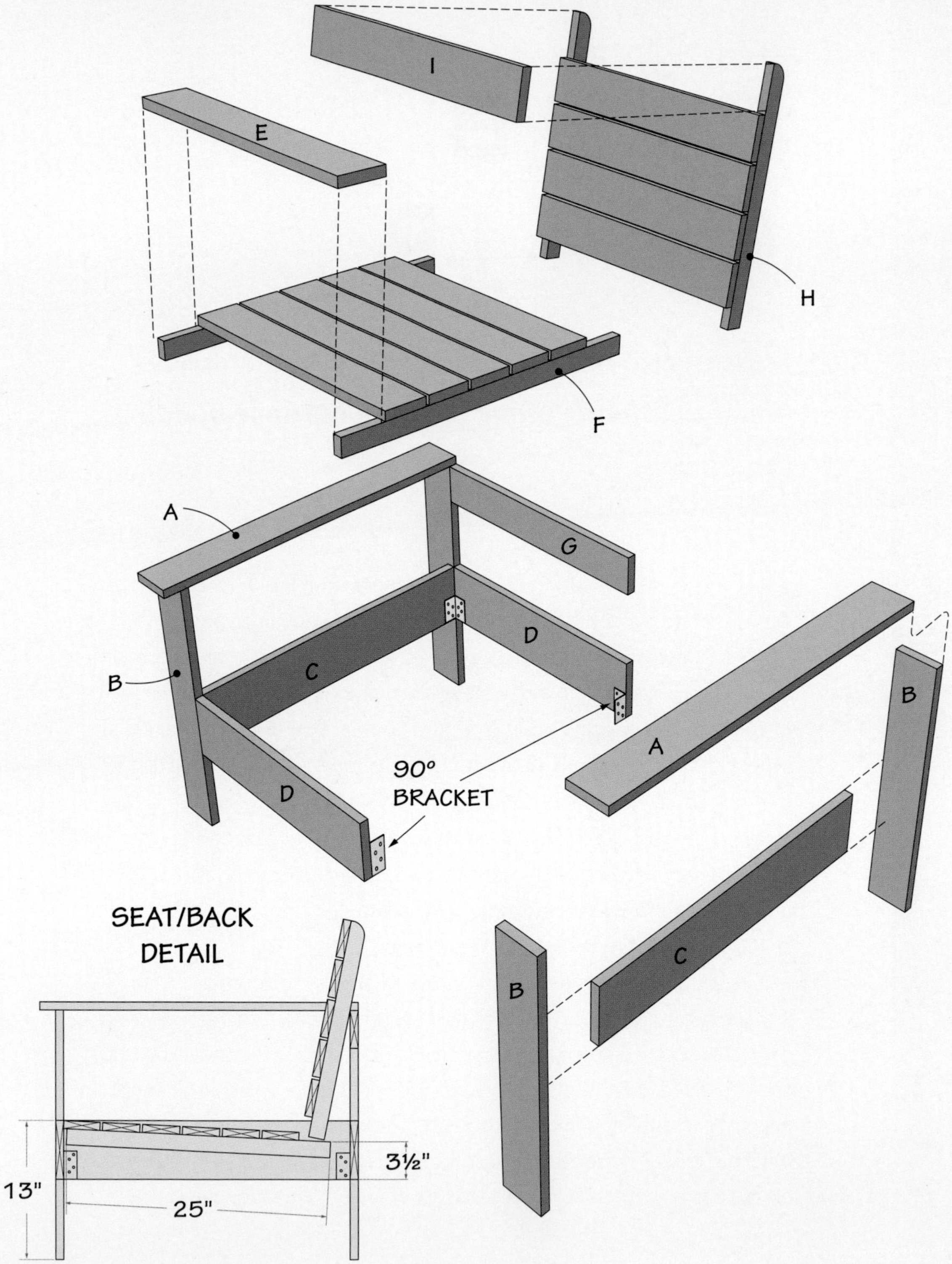

I
E
H
F
A
G
D
C
B
90º
BRACKET
D
A
B
C
B
SEAT/BACK
DETAIL
3½"
13"
25"

Cutting List

Key	Qty	Description	Size
A	2	Arms	¾ x 3½ x 30 in.
B	4	Legs	¾ x 3½ x 23¼ in.
C	2	Side Seat Aprons	¾ x 5½ x 27 in.
D	2	Front/Back Seat Aprons	¾ x 5½ x 21 in.
E	6	Bottom Seat Slats	¾ x 5½ x 21 in.
F	2	Bottom Seat Slat Supports	¾ x 1½ x 25 in.
G	1	Seat Back Cross Support	¾ x 3½ x 21 in.
H	2	Back Seat Slat Supports	¾ x 1½ x 20½ in.
I	5	Back Seat Slats	¾ x 5½ x 21 in.
		Cushion Seat Dimensions: 4 in. T x 24 in. D x 21 in. W	

Materials List

Qty	Description
	(Mahogany or cedar)
5	1 x 4 in. x 8 ft.
1	1 x 6 in. x 10 ft.
1	1 x 2 in. x 8 ft.
	1¼-in. pocket screws
	⅝-in. pan head screws
	1½ x 2¾ in. 90° brackets
	Spar varnish (optional)
	Teak oil (optional)

Tools	
Drill/driver	Straightedge
Tape measure	Level
Square	Clamps
Circular saw	Pocket hole jig
Miter saw	

▶ How to Build a Club Chair

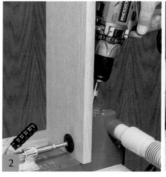

(#1) Cut the arms, legs, and seat aprons to length from 1 x 4 and 1 x 6 stock (we used weather-resistant mahogany).

(#2) Drill pocket holes into the front and rear seat aprons if you are using pocket hole joinery (left photo). Do the same for the side aprons, making sure that your pocket holes are offset or staggered to those on the aprons. This will prevent the screws from hitting each other when the aprons are attached to the legs. Drill two pocket holes into the top of the legs as well. Clamp the legs to the front aprons and attach them with 1¼-inch pocket screws (right photo). Repeat this process for the back apron and legs.

(#3) Clamp the side aprons to the front apron/leg assembly. Making sure that the ends are flush and square, drive pocket screws into the legs. Repeat for the back assembly.

(#4) Turn the chair on its side to attach the arms and legs. Clamp the arms to the front and back legs. The arms should protrude out from the front legs. Drive 1¼-inch pocket screws through the legs and into the arms.

(#5) Attach the seat back cross support between the back legs, securing it with pocket screws.

(#6) Drill holes into the 1 x 2 seat and back slat supports. Pay attention to the spacing in the bottom seat slat supports so you avoid having the fasteners collide when attaching the bottom seat slats, the bottom seat slat supports, and the side aprons.

(#7) Clamp the seat supports to the slats, then drive only one 1¼-inch pocket screw per slat on each end. This allows adjustments to be made to make sure the seat assembly is square. After making any adjustments, reclamp the supports to the slats and drive the second set of screws. This process is repeated for the seat back, with the exception of the side holes.

(#8) Clamp the bottom seat assembly in between the side aprons, following the detail shown in the illustration on page 80, then drive 1¼-inch screws into the aprons.

(#9) Attach the seat back with 1¼-inch screws at the top and bottom of the back seat slat supports, where it meets the arms and side aprons. The seat back slat supports should rest against the seat back cross support.

(#10) Use #8 x ⅝-inch screws to install 90-degree metal brackets at each corner where the aprons and legs meet, providing extra reinforcement to these joints. Apply your finish of choice. We used teak oil to even out the wood tones and top coated with spar varnish.

PALLET TABLE

Whether you call it upcycling, recycling, or repurposing, transforming a wood pallet into a cute table succeeds on many levels

Recycling and reuse go hand in hand with do-it-yourself construction. Beyond the obvious benefit of cost, the materials themselves can spur your imagination and help you generate exciting ideas on how to repurpose them. Pallets have emerged as a good and very popular choice for repurposed building materials. They are plentiful, easy to find, and usually free. Sometimes they are even made of hardwood such as white oak (but usually they are made of something from the pine or spruce family). They are easy to break down into lumber and tend to be reasonably standard when it comes to dimensions.

The project described here was built with just two pallets, with very little leftover. The lumber will likely be of different species—be wary of rot and chemicals, as not all pallets are created equal or used in the same way. Try to use lumber that is similar in size, thickness, and color.

Use caution when disassembling pallets. A hammer and pry bar will likely be all you need, but a reciprocating saw may come in handy on stubborn fasteners. Wear protective eyewear and gloves, and a dust mask if the pallets generate a lot of dust as you break them down.

PALLET TABLE

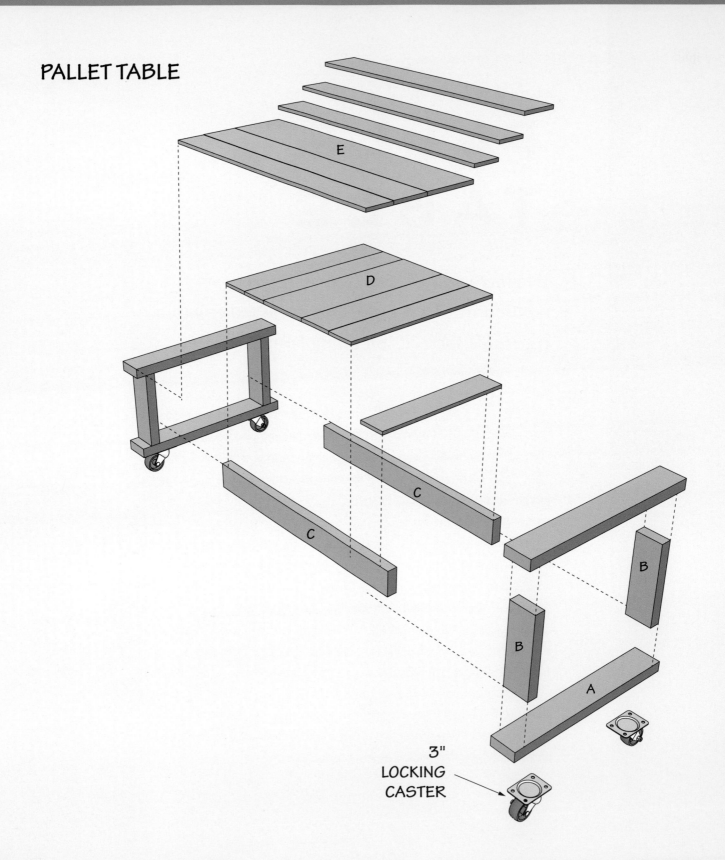

E

D

C

C

B

B

A

3"
LOCKING
CASTER

Cutting List

Key	Qty	Description	Size*
A	4	Top Frames	1½ x 22 in.
B	4	Side Frames	1½ x 10 in.
C	2	Crossbraces	1½ x 30 in.
D	5–7	Shelf Boards	½ x 17 in.
E	5–7	Table Slats	½ x 30½ in.

*Widths vary

Materials List

Qty	Description
3–4	Pallets
	2½-in. deck screws
	1½-in. galvanized finish nails
	Exterior glue
4	3-in. locking casters

Tools	
Drill/driver	Straightedge
Tape measure	Level
Square	Clamps
Circular saw	Paint (optional)

Pallet Recycling

According to the National Wooden Pallet and Container Association, in 2006, over seven billion board feet of lumber was used to manufacture pallets in the United States. Of that, over five billion board feet were recycled by industrial means. That leaves a few left for the handy recyclers. More and more pallets are being creatively reused in a growing number of ways, from furniture to garden planters. A quick search on the web will show you many interesting ways in which people are repurposing them.

You do not have to go far to find them. Pallets can be found in almost any city. Most companies that use them for shipping try to reuse them as much as possible, but there are often imperfect or damaged units that go unused. A recent search online brought up over a dozen places in my area where they can be found for free. Be careful when scrounging—just because a pile of pallets sits in an alley does not make them free for the taking. Find out who they belong to and ask if they are available before you start.

How to Build a Pallet Table

(#1) Disassemble your pallet or pallets and carefully remove any staples or nails. Take stock of your collection of materials to make sure you have enough. Try to find as many boards as possible that are similar in width. Pick out the best pieces for size and appearance.

(#2) Start cutting the pieces to length to make the pallet table parts. Watch out for nails or screws. If you have a scanner that picks up on metal (often a feature of electronic stud finders if they have a wire detection mode), run it over the boards to be safe. An undetected nail can ruin a saw blade.

(#3) Drill countersunk pilot holes in the frames parts at the joints between frame members. The frame members should be made from the thicker internal frame pieces of the pallets (usually around 1½ inches thick), not the thinner pallet slats (usually around ½ inch thick).

(#4) Join the top and side frames into a frame box using 2½-inch deck screws driven into the pilot holes. The horizontal frame members should overhang the vertical members by 1 to 1¼ inches, allowing more accurate construction due to the varying widths of pallet lumber.

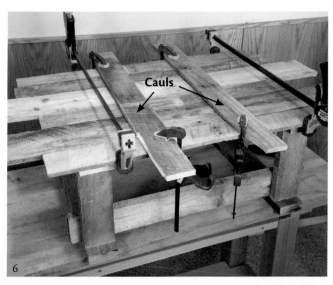

Cauls

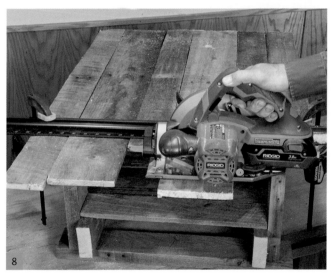

(#5) Attach the frames together with the crossbraces to complete the undercarriage of the table. The crossbraces should extend past the side frames the same amount as in the frame overhang.

(#6) Cut the table slats to rough length, if necessary, and position them on the undercarriage. Move them around for the best fit, then glue and clamp them together edge to edge. Clamp some scrap lumber across the top (a caul) to help the glue-up dry flat.

(#7) Once the glue has dried, remove the cauls and use 1½-inch finish nails to attach the table slats to the top frame. Recess the nail heads below the wood surface with a nail set.

(#8) Using a straightedge and circular saw, trim the table boards on the ragged ends so they are all cut to the same length and the overhangs are equal. Add more boards to the shelf below, cutting them first, then nailing or screwing them to the crossbraces. If you wish to apply a finish, paint is probably your best option. Pallet wood generally does not require a finish, and letting it continue to weather to gray does add to its rustic charm.

TRESTLE DINING TABLE

The *popular farmer's table is reimagined for outdoor dining*

Dining alfresco can turn an everyday meal into an exceptional dining experience. The ambiance nature affords enhances this experience greatly (unless it's raining or the middle of winter, of course). This table is based on a classic trestle farm table. The solid notched posts support a beefy top made of 2 x 6s. A crossbeam stabilizes the legs. A fun feature of the table is its optional serving bin, hidden beneath the center of the table, which provides a well-disguised place to store and serve iced refreshments. It can also serve as a vessel for fresh herbs, flowers, or candles.

If the bin isn't needed, consider drilling a hole to accommodate an umbrella pole. Finish the top with a good spar varnish or pour-on epoxy to keep the table looking good and to help it shed stains.

NOTE: To find the plans for the matching Trestle Dining Benches seen on the opposite page, go to page 95.

TRESTLE DINING TABLE

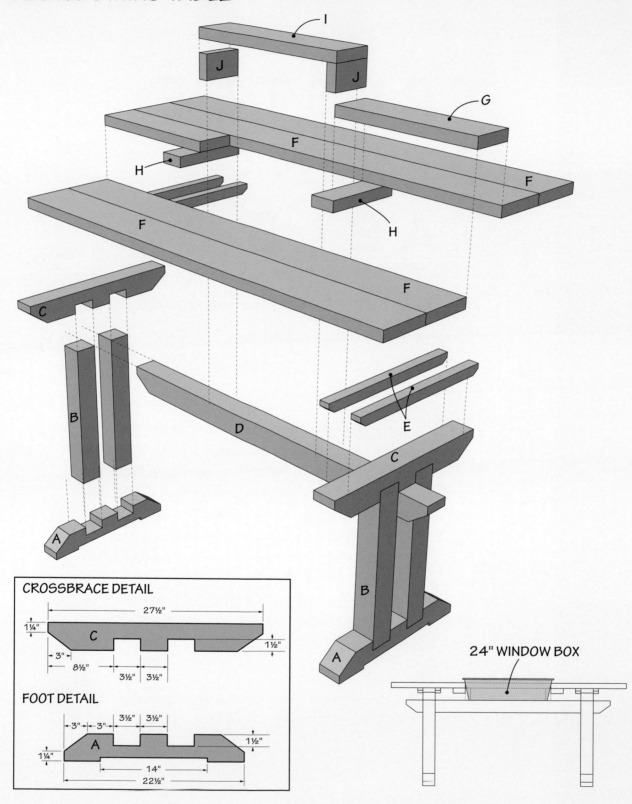

CROSSBRACE DETAIL

27½"

1¼"

C

1½"

3"

8½"

3½" 3½"

FOOT DETAIL

3" 3" 3½" 3½"

1½"

A

1¼"

14"

22½"

24" WINDOW BOX

Cutting List

Key	Qty	Description	Size
A	2	Feet	3½ x 3½ x 25½ in.
B	4	Legs	3½ x 3½ x 23¾ in.
C	2	Upper Supports	3½ x 3½ x 28 in.
D	1	Trestle	3½ x 3½ x 60 in.
E	4	Support Cleats	1½ x 1½ x 33 in.
F	4	Table Planks	1½ x 7¼ x 72 in.
G	2	Center Planks	1½ x 3½ x 25¼ in.
H	2	Center Cleats	1½ x 3½ x 8 in.
I	1	Center Cover	1½ x 3½ x 21½ in.
J	2	Center Cover Legs	½ x 3½ x 3½ in.

Materials List

Qty	Description
	(Cedar or pine)
3	4 x 4-in. x 8 ft.
4	2 x 8-in x 8 ft.
1	2 x 6 in. x 8 ft.
1	2 x 4 in. x 8 ft.
2	2 x 2 in. x 8 ft.
	4-in. deck screws
	2½-in. deck screws
	6-in. timber screws
	24-in. window box planter

Tools	
Drill/driver	Straightedge
Tape measure	Level
Square	Clamps
Circular saw	Chisel

How to Build a Trestle Dining Table

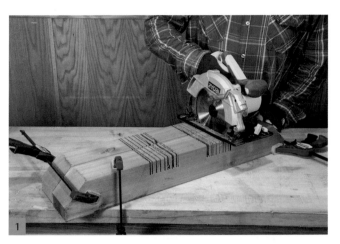

1

Cut the feet and the upper supports from 4 x 4 stock (we used cedar). Make 30-degree profile cuts on the ends, then notch them to accept the legs. See the Foot Detail and Crossbrace Detail illustrations on page 92 for details and measurements. Make the notches by setting your circular saw to a 1½-inch cutting depth and hogging out as much waste wood from the notch area as you can. Take care to get clean, accurate cuts on the shoulders. Remove the remaining wood waste and smooth out the bottoms of the notches with a wood chisel.

2

Cut the legs to length and position them so the tops fit into the notches in the crossbraces and the bottoms fit into the notches in the feet. Make sure everything is good and square and then fasten the parts together with 4-inch exterior-rated screws.

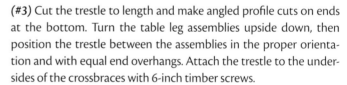

(#3) Cut the trestle to length and make angled profile cuts on ends at the bottom. Turn the table leg assemblies upside down, then position the trestle between the assemblies in the proper orientation and with equal end overhangs. Attach the trestle to the undersides of the crossbraces with 6-inch timber screws.

(#4) The tabletop is formed by edge-gluing two pairs of 2 x 6 planks with a 2 x 4 plank in the center. The center 2 x 4 plank can be split midway to allow for the insertion of a sunken trough that can be put to work as a fun service option. Lay out the tabletop planks on a flat surface with the two 2 x 4 center planks flush at the ends, leaving a 21⅛-inch-long gap in the middle of the table. Glue and clamp the planks together. Stage the leg assembly on top of it. Cut and predrill support cleats, then screw them to the table planks and crossbraces (inset photo). Make sure the planks are flat and square to the frame.

(#5) Attach the center cleats to support the inner ends of the center planks. Then install the center cover cleats at the ends of the opening in the tabletop (see illustration, page 92). Attach two legs to each bottom end of the center cover.

(#6) Turn the table over and inspect it for square and level parts. You may need to trim the ends for a clean finish on the table planks. Sand and apply an exterior-rated finish.

14

TRESTLE DINING BENCH

This beefy bench is designed as an accompaniment for the trestle dining table, but there is no reason it can't stand alone

This bench is designed to accompany the Trestle Dining Table (page 90), but it is also great as extra seating on its own. Its simple construction is sturdy and features the same classic trestle design as the dining table. Its dimensions are easy to modify, so it can become a smaller handy bench for more utilitarian use.

NOTE: Before building this bench on its own, you'll find it useful to review the Trestle Dining Table project on pages 90–94; the construction techniques are very similar.

DINING BENCH

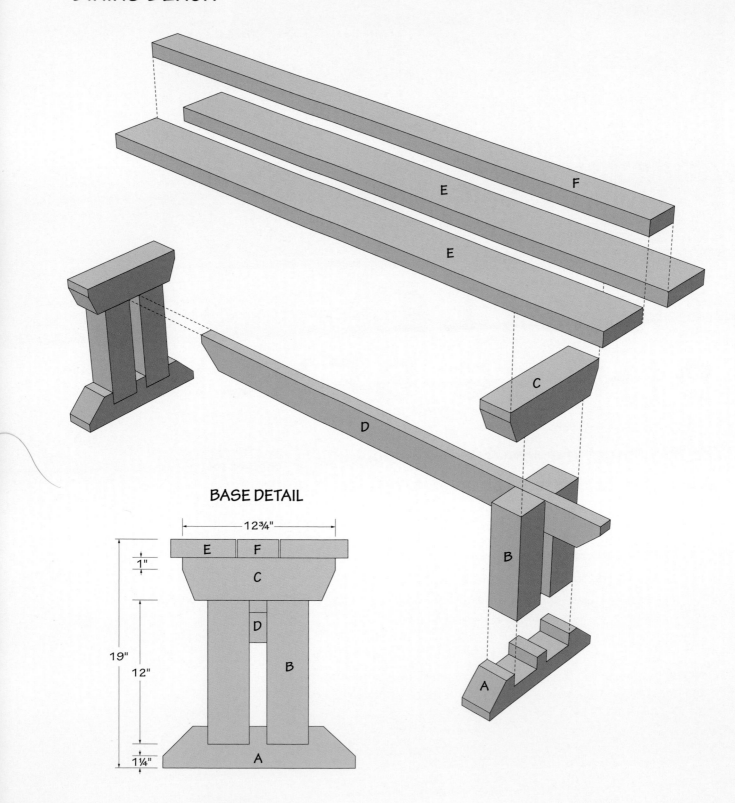

BASE DETAIL

12¾"

E   F

1"

C

19"

12"

B

D

B

A

1¼"

A

Cutting List (One Bench)

Key	Qty	Description	Size
Key	Qty	Description	Size
A	2	Feet	3½ x 3½ x 16 in.
B	4	Legs	3½ x 3½ x 12in.
C	2	Crossbraces	3½ x 3½ x 12¾ in.
D	1	Trestle	1½ x 3½ x 54 in.
E	2	Outer Seat Planks	1½ x 5½ x 60 in.
F	1	Center Seat Plank	1½ x 3½ x 60 in.

Materials List

Qty	Description	Tools	
	(Cedar or pine)	Drill/driver	Circular saw
1	4 x 4 in. x 10 ft.	Tape measure	Clamps
2	2 x 6 in. x 10 ft.	Square	
1	2 x 4 in, x 10 ft.		
	2½-in. deck screws		
	1½-in. trim head screws		
	6-in. timber screws		

How to Make a Trestle Dining Bench

(#1) Cut the feet and the crossbraces to length from 4 x 4 stock, cutting 45- and 22½-degree angles on the ends (see Base Detail opposite page). Notch the feet to accept the legs.

(#2) Clamp the feet, the legs, and the crossbraces together, using a piece of scrap between the legs to hold position for the trestle so you ensure proper spacing. Make sure the crossbrace is centered and then drive 6-inch screws from the feet and crossbraces into the legs.

(#3) Turn the bench legs upside down and then attach the trestle at each end, toe-screwing with 2½-inch deck screws. Drive screws from each side of the trestle.

(#4) Align the seat planks, spacing them no more than ⅛ inch apart, then attach them with 1½-inch trim head stainless-steel screws.

TILED SIDE TABLE

With reverse tapers and a durable tile top, this little table is as versatile as it is handsome

This small, versatile table with style elements borrowed from a classic overhead arbor is the perfect solution when the need arises for some extra entertaining space. It can serve as a refreshment or snack station, or as a companion to a grill when you need somewhere to stage food. The ceramic tile top withstands both hot and cold items and is resistant to moisture. Alternate materials may be used for the top, such as metal, natural stone, or wooden slats. Tapered legs give the table an elegant stance while adding stability. By utilizing pocket-screw joinery, all the fasteners are hidden. You can alter the dimensions to customize the table and add extras like a towel rack, bottle opener, and tool hangers. If you decide to build a larger version, consider using casters to make moving it easier. This is a great project for using up leftover materials. It requires little in the way of lumber and just a few tiles. It's an easy project to build in a single weekend.

Tapering the legs can be done most easily on a table saw, but you can also accomplish the cuts with a circular saw and a tapering jig. By using a jig, your angled cuts will be more accurate. You can use a manufactured jig, but a shop-built tapering jig is easy to make. The diagrams on page 101 show simple jigs for both table and circular saws.

SIDE TABLE

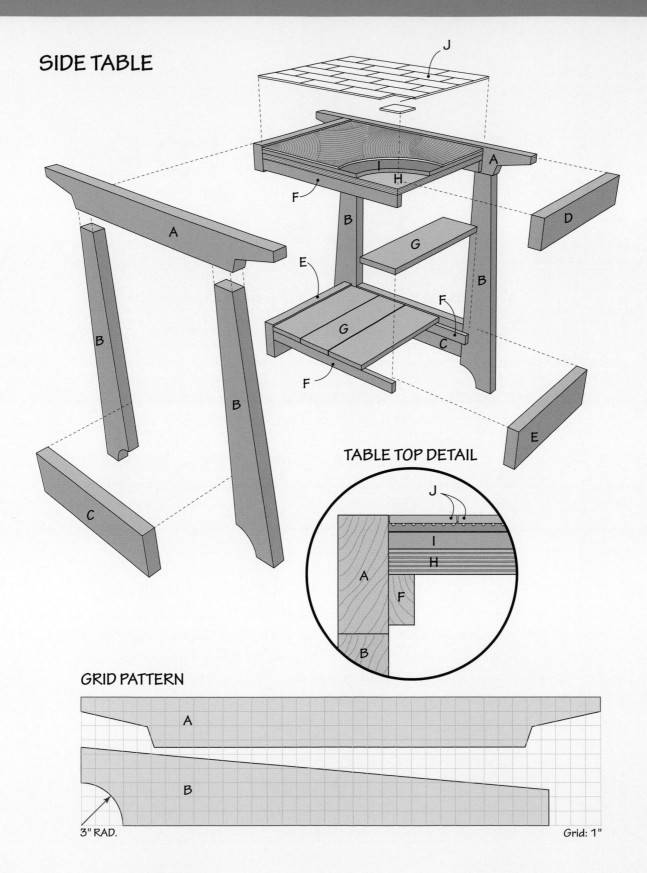

TABLE TOP DETAIL

GRID PATTERN

3" RAD.

Grid: 1"

Cutting List

Key	Qty	Description	Size
A	2	Front/Back Top Rails	1½ x 5½ x 32½ in.
B	4	Legs	1½ x 3½ x 36 in.
C	2	Front/Back Lower Rails	1½ x 5½ x 20 in.
D	2	Left/Right Upper Crossbraces	1½ x 3½ x 18 in.
E	2	Left/Right Lower Crossbraces	1½ x 5½ x 18 in.
F	4	Table Top/Shelf Supports	¾ x 1½ x 20⅞ in.
G	4	Shelf Slats	¾ x 5½ x 18 in.
H	1	Table Underlayment	¾ x 18 x 21 in.
I	1	Cement Board	⅝ x 18 x 21 in.
J	21	Subway Tiles*	¼ x 3 x 6 in. (2.625 sq. ft.)

* Type and size of tile may change required quantity.

Materials List

Qty	Description
	(Cedar or pine)
3	2 x 6 in. x 8 ft.
2	2 x 4 in. x 8 ft.
1	1 x 2 in. x 8 ft.
1	24 x 24 exterior-rated ¾-in. plywood
1	24 x 24 exterior-rated ½-in. cement board
	2½-in. exterior screws or pocket screws
	1½-in. exterior screws
	2-in. exterior screws
	1¼-in. cement board screws
	1½–2 qt. exterior flexible thinset adhesive
	1 qt. grout
	2¾ sq. ft. tile

Tools		
Drill/driver	Tape measure	Square
Circular saw	Clamps	Jigsaw
Notched trowel	Utility knife	

Make a Tapering Jig

Tapering jigs make quick work of creating an elegant table leg (or any other tapered cut). You can build one with scrap wood. There are several designs you can choose from. The diagram below illustrates a simple, easy-to-construct version designed for use with a table saw. For a circular saw, all you really need is a straightedge, but a jig can be just as helpful using hand tools. The circular saw jig shown is simply a framework to hold the workpiece in place while giving the straightedge and saw more stability as the cut is made.

TABLE SAW TAPERING JIG

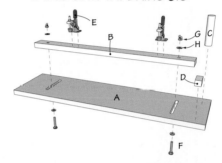

A BASE 8 X 30"
B GUIDE 2½ X 28"
C PUSH HANDLE 1" DIA. X 4½"
D BASE STOP
E VERTICAL TOGGLE CLAMP
F CARRIAGE BOLT
G WINGNUT
H WASHER

CIRCULAR SAW TAPERING JIG

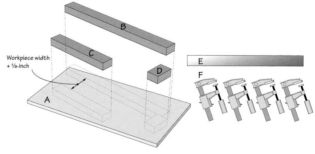

Workpiece width + ⅛-inch

A BASE 18 X 30"
B TOP GUIDE 1½ X 2½ X 28"
C BOTTOM GUIDE 1½ X 2½ X 15"
D END GUIDE 1½ X 2½ X 3½"
E STRAIGHTEDGE MINIMUM 30"
F CLAMPS

How to Build a Tiled Side Table

(#1) Start by cutting the four legs from 2 x 6 cedar boards. The legs are tapered from 5¼ inches at the bottom to 2½ inches at the top. Mark the measurements and rip-cut the boards. A simple jig made from scrap combined with a circular saw and straightedge ensures accurate cuts (see previous page).

(#2) Lay out the profiled ends of the legs. First, make a mark 3 inches up and over from the inside corner of the leg. Draw a 3-inch radius on the inside of the four legs. No compass handy? A roll of tape or a plastic container works as a guide to draw the arc (inset).

(#3) Using a jigsaw, slowly and carefully cut the arcs on the legs. Sand out any imperfections.

(#4) Cut the top rails to length, then lay out and cut the decorative ends with a handsaw or jigsaw. Sand the cut edges smooth. See the Grid Pattern on page 100 for guidance on laying out these cuts.

OPTION: Use a circular saw to get a very straight rail end profile cut. Stop the cut about an inch from the end so as not to overcut, then finish with a handsaw.

(#5) We used pocket screw joinery on much of this project, but if you don't have the jig and bits to make these joints (see page 15), there are other types of joints you can use, including dowel joints, biscuit joints, or even toe-screwing the butt joints to reinforce them. To make pocket screw joints, first drill pocket holes in the inside top end of each of the legs using the pocket hole jig as a guide.

(#6) Cut the two lower rails from 2 x 6 stock. Drill three pocket-screw pilot holes on the inside end of each rail.

(#7) Connect the legs to the lower rails using 2½-inch pocket screws (instead of self-tapping pocket screws, you can use exterior-rated deck screws like those shown).

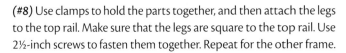

(#8) Use clamps to hold the parts together, and then attach the legs to the top rail. Make sure that the legs are square to the top rail. Use 2½-inch screws to fasten them together. Repeat for the other frame.

(#9) Cut the upper and lower crossbraces from 2 x 4 and 2 x 6 stock, respectively. Drill pocket holes in each end of the crossbraces. Drill two holes into the 2 x 4s and three into the 2 x 6s. Use 2½-inch screws to attach the lower crossbraces to one of the frames. Attach both left and right lower crossbraces.

(#10) Turn the partially assembled frame over, placing it on top of the other frame. Use clamps or scrap lumber to support the top. Drive screws to attach the lower crossbraces to the second frame.

(#11) Place the assembly upright and drive 2½-inch pocket screws to attach the upper crossbraces to the rails. Drive only one screw into each joint.

12

13

14

15

(*#12*) Check for square, measuring the diagonals of the top framework. If the measurements are not the same, adjust as necessary. When the top is square, drive the rest of the screws.

(*#13*) To build the tabletop, first measure 1⅝ to 2 inches down from the top of the frames to allow for the plywood, cement board, thinset, and tile. The tile thickness will determine the total depth required for the tabletop support locations.

(*#14*) The 1 x 2 supports on each of the frames supports the tabletop. Drill pilot holes every 3 to 4 inches through the sides, then drive 1½-inch screws through the supports and into the frames.

(*#15*) Cut an 18 x 20-inch piece of ¾-inch exterior-rated plywood to make the sub-base for the tiled tabletop. This will support the cement board, thinset, and tile.

(#16) Place the plywood sub-base into the top frame and secure it by driving 1½-inch screws through the plywood and into the 1 x 2 supports.

(#17) Using a carbide-tipped utility knife, or a jigsaw and specialty blade for cutting cement board, cut an 18 x 20-inch piece of ¾-inch-thick cement board.

(#18) Screw the cement board down to the plywood using 1¼-inch cement board screws (you could also use deck screws, but cement board screws are designed to tap through the dense cement board without a pilot hole).

(#19) Before you set any tiles, dry-set the tile layout to make sure that you have enough and that it will fit the 18 x 20-inch top. If you are using standard-size tiles, you should be able to achieve the layout without needing to cut any tiles. Then, following the manufacturer's instructions, mix a small amount (about 2 quarts) of flexible thin-set adhesive. With a ¼-inch notched trowel, spread a bed of thinset onto the top of the cement board.

TIP: Before tiling, tape off the top of the table frames with painter's masking tape to protect them from becoming stained by the thinset or grout.

(#20) Unlike laying a larger tile job from the center, start at the top left and work your way down and to the right with the tile. Most tiles today have cast-in spacing numbs on the edges, but if yours don't, insert tile spacers in all joints so you get uniform spacing. If you are using a typical running bond layout, as seen here, you'll need to cut a few tiles in half to set them with staggered joint lines (some tile comes with half-tiles available).

ALTERNATIVE: Instead of smallish wall tile or subway like we used, you could use just a single large slab of floor tile. A single 24 x 24-inch tile can be cut to fit perfectly and requires no grout, as a bead of caulk around the outside will suffice to seal it.

(#21) Allow the thinset to dry for a day or two, and then grout the tile, following the manufacturer's instructions. Allow the grout to dry for another 24 hours, then buff the tile surface and remove the masking tape.

(#22) Carefully turn the table on its side. To install the lower shelf, use pre-drilled, countersunk 1½-inch strips as supports. Attach the supports to the frame, using 1½-inch screws.

(#23) Hide the screws by fastening the shelf slats from the bottom, driving 2-inch screws up through the supports and into the shelf slats.

16

INDUSTRIAL SNACK BAR

Add a little bit of industrial chic to your outdoor entertaining with this handy snack bar

Having a dedicated place for serving food and drinks is a good idea for any deck or patio, and building one is easy. This project is as functional as it is funky. The materials give it an on-trend industrial appearance. The construction is straightforward and most of the project can be completed in a single afternoon, with some simple preparation.

The countertop may be constructed from just about any material you choose, from concrete to metal or even tile, as long as it will stand up to the elements. The top shown is an edge-glued pine panel. But be careful not to overload the structure with a heavy top, which could make it prone to tipping.

Finish the snack bar off with paint, fun decals, or give it a distressed look. You can replace the corrugated metal panels with bamboo and reed fencing and go for a tiki-inspired feel. Or go with a western style and use logs and wagon wheels. Whichever style you choose, this project will be the center of fun and function for your deck or patio.

NOTE: The two stools you see in the photo (opposite page) are made with galvanized pipe, which complements the corrugated metal panels nicely. To build them, see Galv-Pipe Stool on page 114.

SNACK BAR

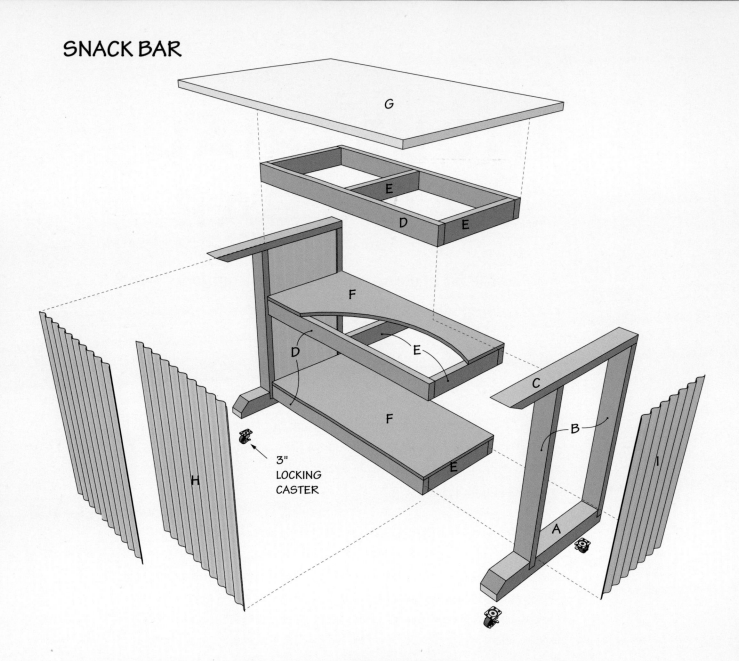

G

E

D

E

F

D

E

F

E

C

B

A

3"
LOCKING
CASTER

H

I

FOOT DETAIL (A)

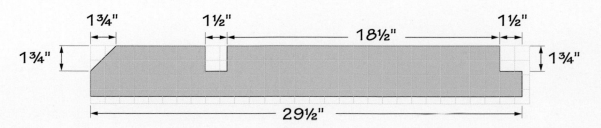

1¾"

1½"

18½"

1½"

1¾"

1¾"

29½"

Cutting List

Key	Qty	Description	Size
A	2	Feet	3½ x 3½ x 29½ in.
B	4	Legs	1½ x 3½ x 35½ in.
C	2	Top Supports	1½ x 3½ x 28 in.
D	6	Front/Back Shelf Supports	1½ x 3½ x 46 in.
E	9	Side Shelf Supports	1½ x 3½ x 18 in.
F	2	Shelves	¾ x 21 x 46 in.
G	1	Table Top	1½ x 30 x 60 in.
H	2	Metal Panels	2 x 26 x 37 in.
I	2	Metal Panels	2 x 26 x 33⅝ in.

Materials List

Qty	Description
	(Cedar)
1	4 x 4 in. x 8 ft.
7	2 x 4 in. x 8 ft.
1	1 x 2 in. x 8 ft.
1	48 x 96 exterior-rated ¾-in. plywood
	1 x 30 x 60 edge-glued panel
	1 x 26 x 8 ft. corrugated metal panel
	2½-in. exterior-rated deck screws
	1½-in. stainless-steel screws
4	3-in. locking casters
	Clear top coat

Tools	
Aviation snips	Square
Drill/driver	Circular saw
Tape measure	Clamps
Awl or hammer	

How to Build an Industrial Snack Bar

(#1) Cut the two feet to length from 4 x 4 stock (we used cedar). Cut 45-degree chamfers on the front end of the feet to lighten them visually and to reduce the possibility of tripping. Create 1½-inch deep notches in the top and at one end of each foot to accept the front and back legs. See Foot Detail, page 110.

TIP: Make a sanding block the same width as your notches and use it to smooth out the bottoms of the notches so you get a clean, flush joint.

(#2) Cut the top supports, adding a 45-degree chamfer cut to the fronts to match the chamfers on the feet. Attach the legs and top supports to the feet to form a solid frame. Make sure all planes are level, plumb, and square.

(#3) Cut the shelf supports (front, back, and side) from 2 x 4 stock. Attach them together to form frames using 2½-inch exterior-rated deck screws to make the joints. You can add one, two, or even three shelves, depending on your needs.

(#4) Starting at the bottom, clamp the shelf support frames to the foot framing, adjust for level and plumb, then drive 2½-inch countersunk deck screws to fasten the parts together.

(**#5**) Add the top shelf to the assembly and again adjust for level and plumb. Join the parts with deck screws. Add any additional cross supports if you'd like additional shelves.

(**#6**) Measure, mark, and cut the corrugated metal panels with a straight aviation snip. You can find corrugated roofing panels like the ones seen here in the roofing supplies department of your local building center. (Or you can choose a different option for these panels—see the discussion on page 109.) Wear gloves and safety goggles when working with and cutting metal.

(**#7**) Clamp the panels in place and screw them to the frame using 1½-inch stainless-steel screws. To make driving the screws easier, punch small starter holes in the metal with an awl or with a hammer and a small finish nail.

(**#8**) Attach the top using 2½-inch stainless-steel screws driven through the top supports. We used a glued-up pine panel purchased at the building center and finished it with a clear exterior-rated top coat.

17

GALV-PIPE STOOL

You don't need to be a professional pipefitter to fabricate these fun outdoor stools

This is a companion project to the Industrial Snack Bar (pages 108 to 113). Its metal and wood design is meant to complement that particular project, but you can use this stool in many other ways and with other tables or bars. Or simply keep them around to provide extra seating when needed.

Black or galvanized pipe can be used for this project, but be wary—black pipe will quickly rust when left outdoors unless it has been treated with a sealer and exterior paint. Galvanized pipe will resist rust but is not impervious to it. It too should be sealed and/or painted to maximize protection from the elements (see Painting Galvanized Pipe on page 117).

You don't need any special pipefitting equipment to fabricate these metal stool bases. The joints are made with threaded pipe fittings, so all you need is a decent pipe wrench or two to get everything good and snug.

115

PIPE STOOL

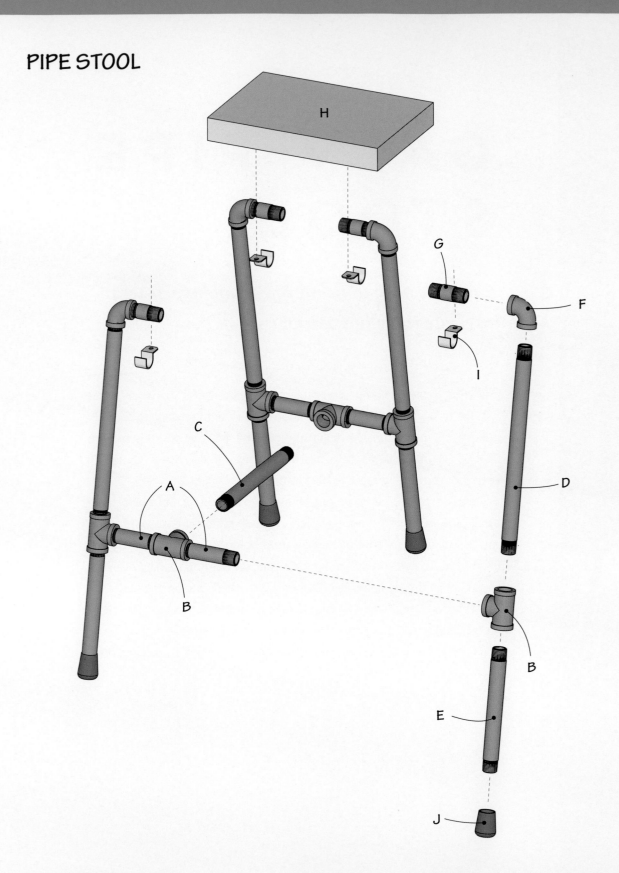

Cutting List (One Stool)

Key	Qty	Description	Size
A	4	Leg Crossbraces	¾ dia. x 5 in.
B	6	T-Joints	¾ dia.
C	1	Center Crossbrace	¾ dia. x 12 in.
D	4	Upper Legs	¾ dia. x 18 in.
E	4	Lower Legs	¾ dia. x 10 in.
F	4	90° Elbows	¾ dia.
G	4	Seat Supports	¾ dia. x 4 in.
H	1	Seat	2 x 9 x 12 in.
I	4	Pipe Straps	1½ in.
J	4	Rubber Chair Feet	

Materials List

Qty	Description
	(All pipe ¾-in. diameter)
4	4 in.
2	5 in.
4	10 in.
1	12 in.
4	18 in.
6	Tee
4	90° elbow
4	Caps
	1½-in. conduit/pipe straps
	#10 x 1-in. lag screws
	2 x 10 in. x 1 ft. pine, cedar, or maple
	Pipe dope

Tools		
Pipe wrenches/locking pliers	Drill/driver	Tape measure
Square	Circular saw	Clamps

Painting Galvanized Pipe

Galvanized metal does not take paint well. It may seem to look good at first, but eventually the paint will fail, peeling away from the metal. But you can get the paint to hold if you prepare the metal properly. Start by cleaning the metal with soap and water, rinsing it, and allowing it to dry. Apply a weak solution of ammonia and water, letting it dry as well. Finally, sand the metal completely. Be sure to wear protective gear, including a NIOSH-approved respirator, when sanding or grinding galvanized metal—the zinc galvanized finish can give off harmful vapors and particulates. Wipe the surface clean with tack cloths.

Starting at the top, spray a metal primer coat. Finish with metal paint, following the manufacturer's instructions. Applying multiple thin coats will result in a more durable, better-quality finish than one or two heavier coats.

This stool is designed to be built with stock lengths of threaded galvanized pipe, so if you follow the plan (and your local building center has a good inventory of threaded pipe, nipples, and fittings), you should be able to get by without needing to cut any pipes. Gather all of the parts, including the pipe and connectors, along with two pipe wrenches. A vise can act as a second pair of hands and will make screwing the parts together easier.

How to Build a Galv-Pipe Stool

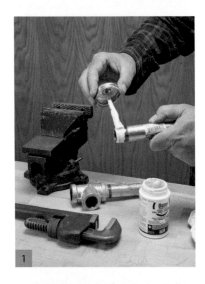

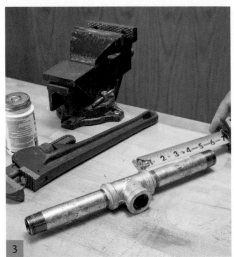

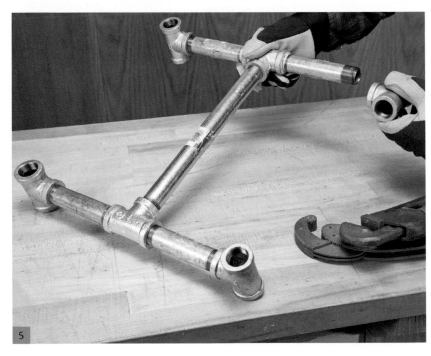

(#1) While it is not mandatory to use pipe dope, you may find it easier to wrench the fittings together tightly, as the main purpose of pipe dope is to lubricate the joints, not to seal them. It will also ease the disassembly of pipe fittings if you should need to take them apart.

(#2) Start assembling from the inside and work outward. Screw the leg crossbraces into the opposite ends of the tee fitting.

(#3) Measure the leg crossbraces on each side, making sure they are the same, and then repeat with the second leg crossbrace assembly.

(#4) Screw the center crossbrace into each of the leg crossbraces at the center tee fitting.

(#5) Screw four tee fittings onto the outside ends of the leg crossbraces.

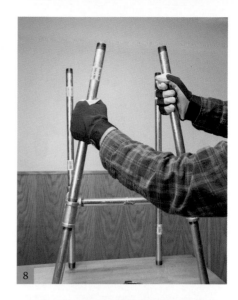

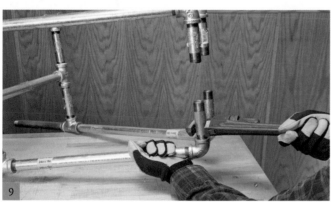

(*#6*) Insert the four upper legs sections into the four tee fittings.

(*#7*) Turn the assembly upside down, then screw the four lower leg sections to the bottom ends of the tee fittings.

(*#8*) Holding the upper leg sections, carefully pull the opposite sides toward one another until the tops of the pipes are approximately 12 inches apart.

(*#9*) Screw the seat supports into the four 90-degree elbows, then screw the elbows to the upper leg sections.

(*#10*) Cut the seat top from 2 x 12 stock, or use recycled materials, such as this butcher-block scrap.

(*#11*) Use 1½-inch pipe straps to attach the seat to the framework with #10 x 1-inch lag screws. Apply a finish to the seat and to the stool base (See page 117).

LOW-BACK FOLDING CHAIR

Make several of these comfy chairs and keep them hanging around until they're needed

There was a time in history when owning a folding chair was considered a prized possession, a symbol of status. They were used in rituals, formal ceremonies, and important events dating back thousands of years. Today they are just as handy as ever, and when you need extra seating, they are a convenient furnishing to have on hand.

This design is incredibly easy to build and has a small footprint when folded. They can be hung on a wall and stacked horizontally. The low back is perfect for formal or casual occasions, and they can be built and finished in virtually any style of lumber. ⁵⁄₄ x 6 cedar boards are used here, and the extra thickness over standard 1x lumber is a good idea for sturdiness and stability. Use brass screws for a classy finish.

121

FOLDING CHAIR

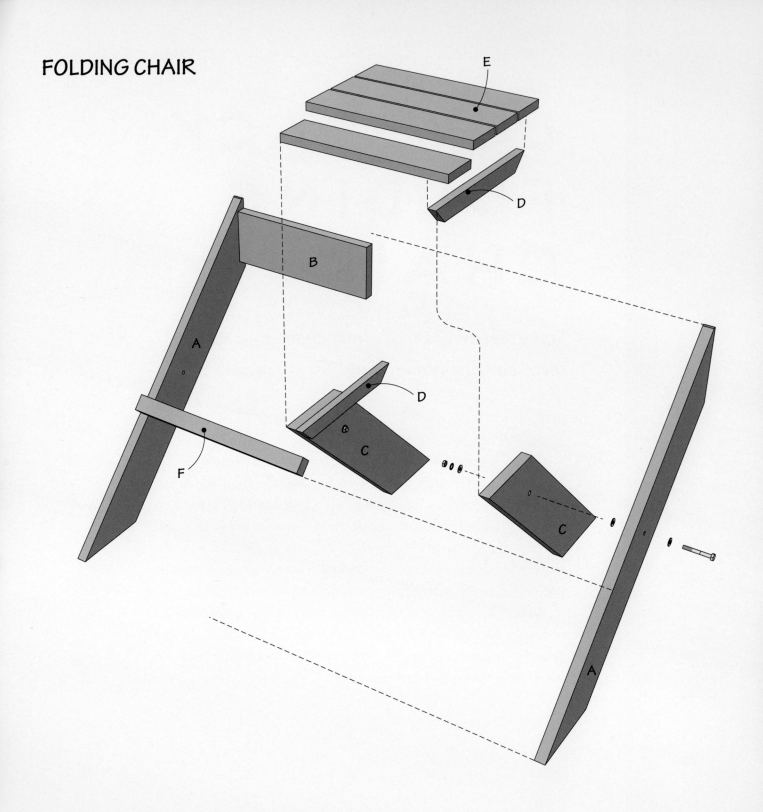

Cutting List (One Chair)

Key	Qty	Description	Size
A	2	Front Legs	5/4 x 5½ x 39½ in.
B	1	Seat Back	5/4 x 5½ x 18 in.
C	2	Back Legs	5/4 x 5½ x 29½ in.
D	2	Seat Supports	1½ x 1½ x 14¾ in.
E	4	Seat Slats	¾ x 3½ x 17¾ in.
F	1	Seat Stop	1½ x 1½ x 20 in.

Materials List

Qty	Description
	(Cedar)
2	5/4 x 6 in. x 8 ft.
1	2 x 2 in. x 8 ft.
1	1 x 4 in. x 8 ft.
	1½-in. brass screws
	2½-in. deck screws
2	¼ x 2½-in. stainless-steel carriage bolts
6	¼-in. washers
2	¼-in. lock washers
2	¼-in. nuts
	Loctite

Tools	
Drill/driver	Square
Tape measure	Clamps
Circular saw	Adjustable wrench
Torpedo level	

CENTERPOINT

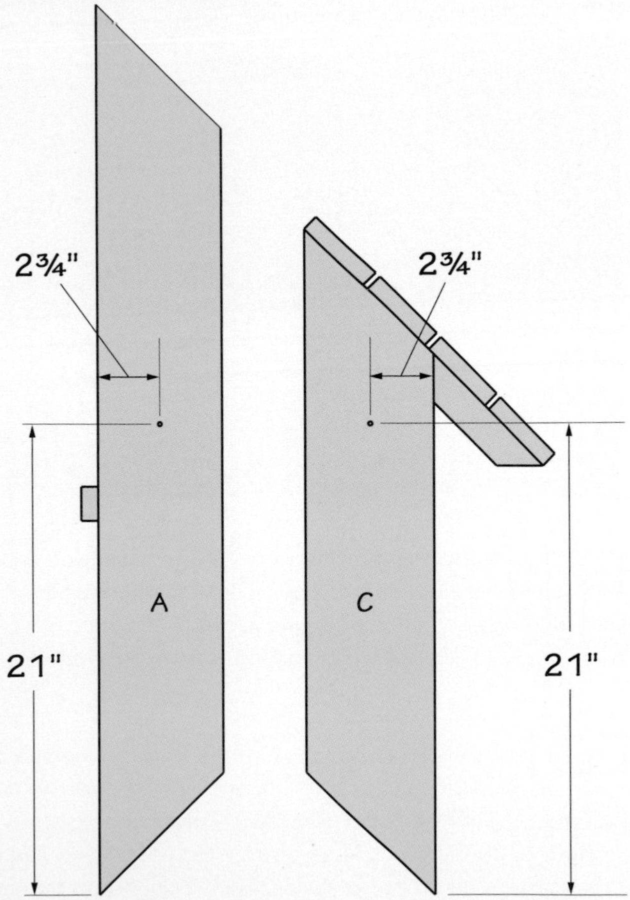

2¾"   2¾"

A   C

21"   21"

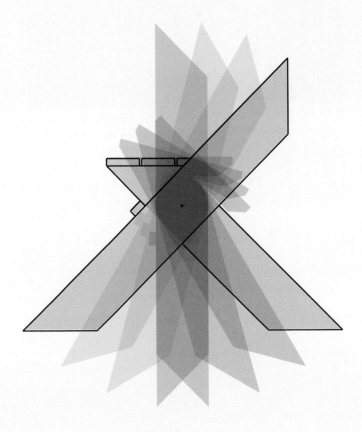

▶ How to Build a Low-Back Folding Chair

(#1) Cut the front and back legs to length. We used cedar decking boards that are dimensioned at ⁵/₄ x 6 inches. Make parallel 45-degree miter cuts at the ends of the boards (see Centerpoint Drawings, page 123).

(#2) Cut the seat back to length and position it between the two front legs. Clamp the boards together and drive 1½-inch brass screws into countersunk pilot holes.

(#3) Cut the two seat supports from 2 x 2 stock, mitering the ends at 45 degrees. Drill several counterbored pilot holes in the underside of each support, and then use 2½-inch screws to attach the supports to the insides of the back legs, making sure the mitered ends are flush at the front.

(#4) Cut the seat slats to length. Turn the front legs on end and clamp the seat slats to the seat supports, spacing them about ¼ inch apart. Drill countersunk pilot holes then attach the slats to the supports by driving two 1½-inch brass screws at each end. Position these screws to miss those attaching the seat supports to the legs.

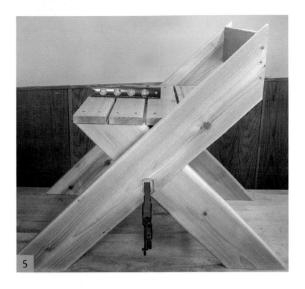

(#5) Clamp the front and back legs together in the open position, checking for fit. Set a torpedo level on the seat to make sure it is level. Mark centered drilling points on the legs for the bolt that will be installed in each leg pair to create the "hinge." See diagram, page 123.

(#6) With the legs set in the closed position, drive a small screw through the inside of the back leg and into the front leg to pin the assembly together temporarily. Unfold the chair and recheck the angle and fit. Repeat this process if needed, adjusting the centerpoint if you are not happy with the fit.

(#7) Open the chair, making sure that the legs are flat on the workbench. Clamp the legs together. Use 2½-inch screws to attach the seat stop to the front legs so that it makes contact with the back legs. If the back legs are splayed or warped, add an optional crossbrace near the bottom.

(#8) Keeping the chair securely clamped, remove the temporary screws and drill a ¼-inch hole through both the front and back legs. Drill from the outside of the front legs so that any drill tearout will not be visible. Insert a ¼ inch diameter 2½-inch stainless-steel carriage bolt through the hole toward the inside of the legs. Place a stainless-steel washer on the bolt end before pushing it through the back leg to create a pivot/spacer. Then push the bolt through the back leg and attach a washer, lock washer, and nut. Use a thread locker like Loctite or a similar product to keep the nut from loosening over time as the chair is unfolded. Do not overtighten the nut. Sand the edges and the top corners and finish as desired.

PATIO-DOOR ARBOR

Get all the beauty and functionality of an overhead arbor without sacrificing a single square foot of floor space

Arbors are a wonderful architectural accent that can add beauty to your home. Using one over an entryway defines the space, adds character, and filters sunlight. The problem is, most overhead arbors require at least two support posts, and that can cut your deck living space significantly. But because this arbor is actually meant to be wall mounted, you can hang it over your patio door and keep the full amount of clear space on the deck or patio below.

The arbor dimensions can be adjusted to fit just about any exterior or patio door, and the project can be easily built in a weekend. This design utilizes saddle joinery for stability, style, and strength. Finish it with a stain to match your structure, or add a contrasting color to make it more dynamic.

This project can also be adapted to fit over a garage door or windows to block troublesome direct sunlight, and it can be built using natural or composite materials. When you're finished, add design details like lighting, plantings, and hanging garden art.

PATIO-DOOR ARBOR

RAFTER DETAIL (C)

1½"
1³⁄₈"
3½"
6¼"
7"
11"
¾"

D

B

B

A

C

C

B

BRACKET DETAIL (B)

18"
9"
1½"
2½"
¾"
1½"
5½"
1½"
¾"
4"

110"
55"
11"
2¾"
43¼"
46"
92"

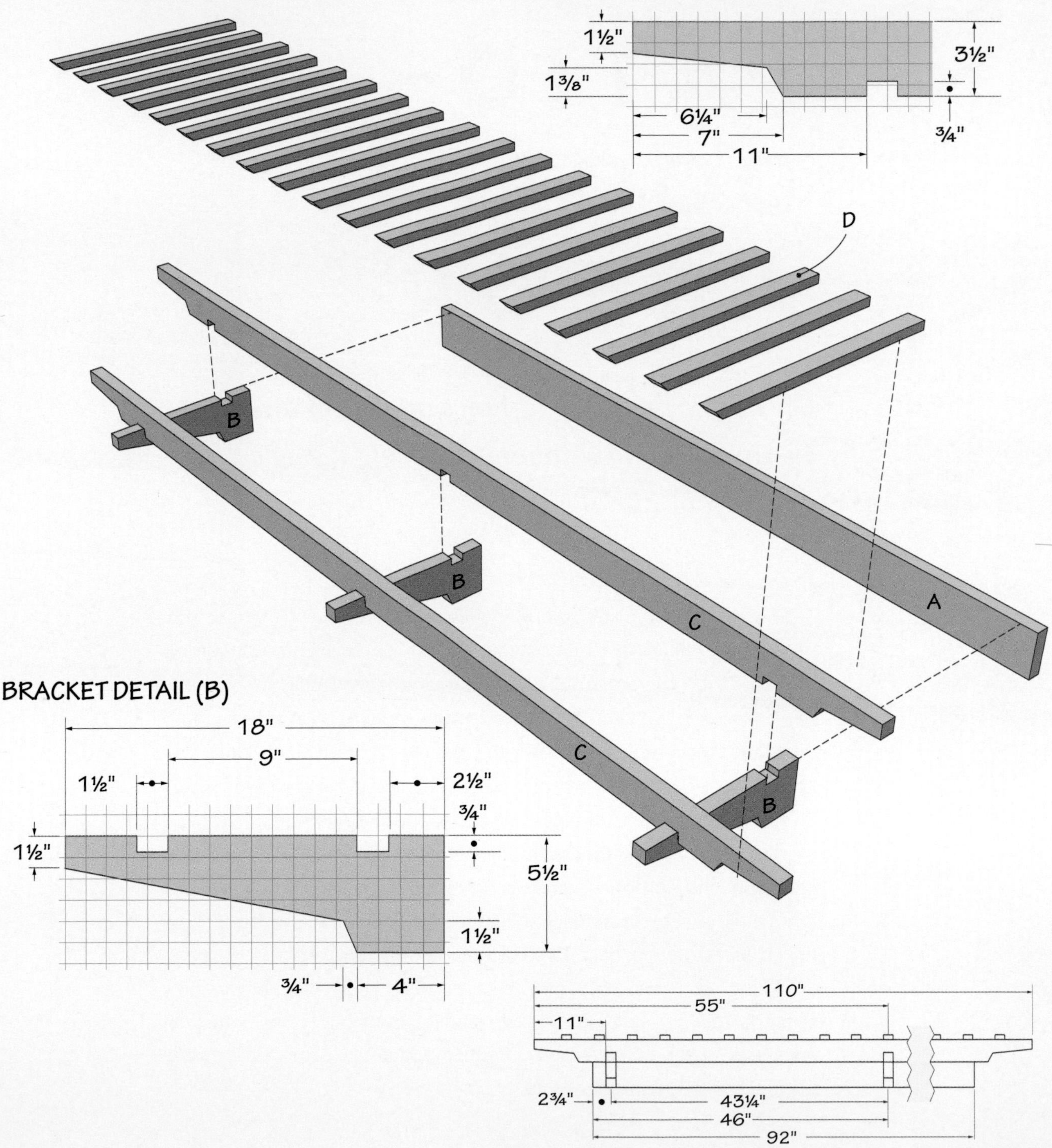

Cutting List

Key	Qty	Description	Size
A	1	Ledger	1½ x 5½ x 92 in.
B	3	Brackets	1½ x 5½ x 18 in.
C	2	Rafters	1½ x 3½ x 110 in.
D	19	Purlins	1½ x 1½ x 21 in.

Materials List

Qty	Description
	(Cedar or pine)
2	2 x 6 in. x 8 ft.
2	2 x 4 in. x 10 ft.
5	1 x 2 in. x 8 ft.
	4-in. deck screws
	2½-in. deck screws
	1¼-in. deck screws
	4- to 6-in. timber screws
	Oil stain or paint (optional)

Tools	
Drill/driver	Circular saw
Tape measure	Chisel
Square	Clamps
Handsaw	Stud finder
Wiring detector	

▶ How to Build a Patio-Door Arbor

(#1) Cut the ledger support and three brackets to length from 2 x 6 stock, then gang the brackets together with clamps and notch them (see Bracket Detail, page 128). To cut the notches, set your circular saw to a ¾-inch cutting depth and make multiple passes over the notch cutout area to remove as much wood waste as you can. Finish the cuts with a wood chisel and sand the bottoms smooth, if necessary.

(#2) Cut the decorative angle into the brackets with a circular saw, stopping a few inches from the end. Finish the cut with a handsaw. Sand the parts.

(#3) Cut the two rafters that run the full width of the arbor from 2 x 4 stock. Carefully measure and mark the locations for the three brackets. Make notches in the bottoms of the two rafters to align with the bracket notches. Cut a decorative end profile on each end of the rafters. Sand the parts.

(#4) The arbor is supported by a 2 x 6 ledger that will be bolted to the house framing much like a deck ledger is. Cut the ledger to length and then measure and mark the bracket locations onto the ledger.

(#5) Clamp the brackets to the ledger in their marked positions. Drive at least three 4-inch deck screws through the back of the ledger and into the end of each bracket to fasten it.

6

7

8

Watch Out for Wires

Before you drill or screw into any wall, make certain there is no wiring or plumbing in the wall cavity where you are working. In this project, because patio doors typically have an exterior light or two above the door as well as an interior light switch near the door on the inside, you are almost certain to find electrical cables running next to the door opening inside the wall. There is a good like-lihood you'll discover cables above the door header, particularly if you have an exterior light on each side of the door. It is a very good idea to purchase a handheld wiring detector (similar to a stud detector) and test the work area. If wiring is present, choose a higher or lower location for the arbor.

Always turn off the electrical power at the main service panel before cutting or drilling into a wall.

(#6) Test-fit the rafters to the brackets to make sure that the saddle joints align. Use a mallet to carefully mate the parts, and then use 2½-inch deck screws to join them. Drive the screws diagonally from the backside of the rafters and into the brackets.

(#7) The purlins are the 2 x 2 strips that mount at the top of the arbor, perpendicular to the house. Cut the purlins to length, then, starting at the middle and using a square and a block of wood for spacing, attach them to the rafters with 2½-inch screws. Cut 30-degree angles at the ends of the purlins.

(#8) Finish the arbor with an oil stain, leave it natural, or paint it to match your house trim. To mount the arbor on your exterior house wall, use a stud detector to locate cripple studs behind the exterior wall covering. You need to attach the ledger to framing members, not just the wall sheathing. In some cases, you may be able to attach it to the header in the wall above the door opening, but this will leave you little or no space between the top of the exterior door casing or brick-mold and the bottom of the ledger (a little space is a nice visual break). Find and mark the framing member locations and then measure and transfer them to the outside face of the ledger so you know where to drill to hit the framing members.

Get a minimum of two helpers to assist you in raising and installing the arbor. You can use lag screws or timber screws to mount the structure (don't use any that are longer than 6 inches, as that could penetrate the interior wall covering). Start the screws before you lift the arbor into position. Use ladders and carefully hoist it into position. Shut off electrical power. Once the arbor is in position, drive 4- to 6-inch timber screws to fasten it to the framing members of the wall. A spacer behind the ledger board may be required, depending on the siding type.

PRIVACY PLANTER

Keep the sun and wind (and nosy neighbors) out of your space with this screen and planter combo

There are times that you may feel like your little piece of peace and quiet is a bit too much on display. That's when a privacy screen is the perfect addition to a deck, patio, or balcony. In addition to privacy, a screen can protect from sun and wind. The screen shown here can do all that and more—this screen is also built to hold plants. The lattice panel is the perfect structure for climbing vines. Standard 24-inch window-box-style planters are integrated into the design. This planter is also mobile and can easily be moved wherever it is needed. Casters can be installed, or simply adding padding like carpet to the underside of the base will make the screen easier to move about.

A heavier base supports a lighter, open screen, which allows wind to pass through, making it less likely to tip. But if strong winds are common in your area, consider permanently attaching the privacy planter to a structure.

Using flower boxes with drip trays will help keep your deck or patio clean and free of excess water runoff. Once plants are established, you'll have a screen that provides privacy while being a beautiful backdrop for your favorite flowers or veggies.

PRIVACY PLANTER

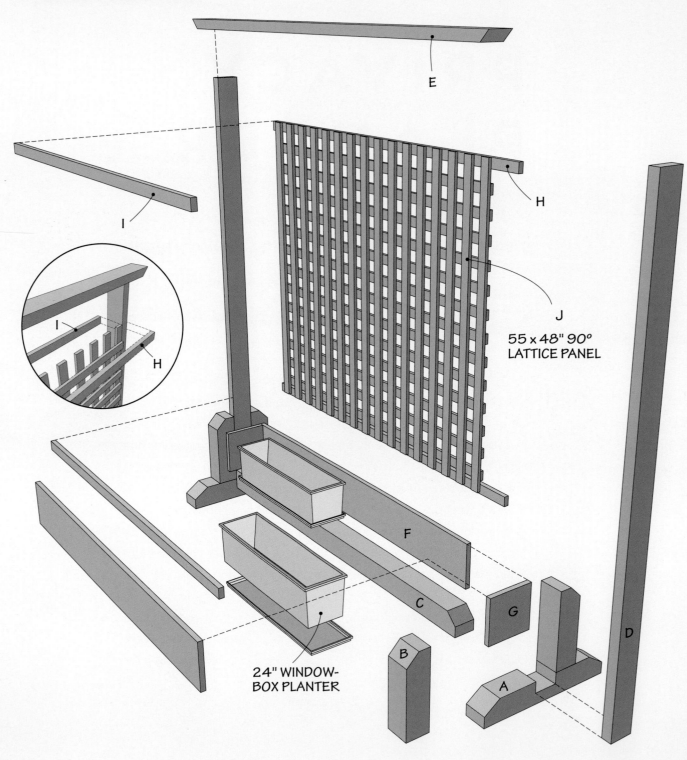

E

I

H

J

55 x 48" 90°
LATTICE PANEL

F

C

G

D

B

A

24" WINDOW-
BOX PLANTER

Cutting List

Key	Qty	Description	Size
A	2	Feet	3½ x 3½ x 24 in.
B	4	Upright Supports	3½ x 3½ x 12 in.
C	1	Cross Beam	1/1-2 x 3½ x 68 in.
D	2	Uprights	1½ x 3½ x 72 in.
E	1	Lintel	1/1-2 x 3½ x 82 in.
F	2	Box Panels	¾ x 7¼ x 57 in.
G	2	Box End Panels	¾ x 7¼ x 7¼ in.
H	2	Outside Trim Strips	¾ x 1½ x 60 in.
I	2	Inside Trim Strips	¾ x 1½ x 57 in.
J	1	90° Lattice Panel	¾ x 48 x 55 in.

Materials List

Qty	Description
	(Cedar)
2	4 x 4 in. x 8 ft.
3	2 x 4 in. x 8 ft.
4	1 x 2 in. x 8 ft.
2	1 x 8 in. x 8 ft.
	1½-in. deck screws
	2½-in. deck screws
	6-in. deck screws
	1½-in. trim head screws
2	Window-box planters

Tools	
Drill/driver	Circular saw
Tape measure	Clamps
Square	Chisel

▶ How to Build a Privacy Planter

(**#1**) Create the feet by cutting a 4 x 4 post (we used cedar) to 24-inch lengths. Add a decorative 45-degree angled miter on each end. Cut a 3½-inch notch in the center to accept the crossbeam by first kerfing with a circular saw set at 2 inches cutting depth and then finishing the notches with a wood chisel. You'll get faster, more accurate results if you clamp the two posts together while tooling them as one unit.

(**#2**) Turn the pieces over for easier attaching. Lay the crossbeam top-edge down on a flat worksurface, set into the notches you cut on the feet. The beam should overhang each foot by 2½ inches. Drive 4-inch deck screws through the feet and into the crossbeam.

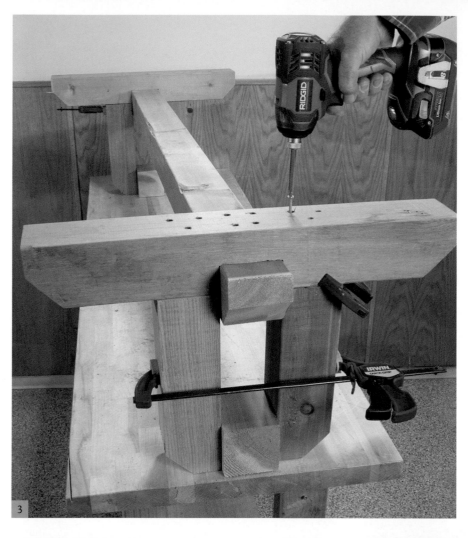

(#3) Cut the upright supports to length and then cut a matching 45-degree miter at the top of each support. Lay a couple of pieces of 4 x 4 scrap on your worksurface to use as spacers between the upright supports. Set the supports top-end down on the worksurface and then clamp them together around each spacer. Lay the cross-beam/foot assembly onto the ends of the supports and clamp it in place. Attach the supports to the beam by driving a 6-inch screw down through the feet and into the ends of the upright supports. Strengthen these connections with two more screws per joint.

(#4) Measure the distance between the upright supports, and then transfer that dimension to the lintel (the top rail), centering it between the uprights. The lintel should overhang each upright by 11 inches.

(#5) Drive 2½-inch deck screws through the lintel to the top ends of the uprights to join the parts together. Double-check to make sure the overhangs are equal.

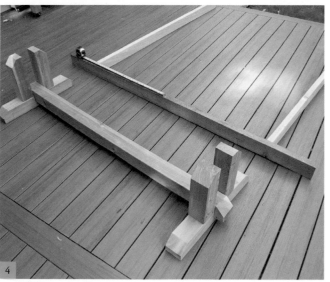

(#6) Set the upright and lintel assembly into the upright supports with the uprights between the supports, flush with the inside surfaces. Drive 2½-inch deck screws at an angle to attach them.

(#7) Cut the panels for the planting box from 1 x 8 cedar. Assemble the planter box by attaching the box panels to the box panel ends with trim head screws or nails. Fit the box between them upright, then drive 1½-inch deck screws through the box panel ends into the upright supports. The crossbeam acts as a bottom for the box.

(#8) Using 1½-inch deck screws, attach the outer trim strips to the uprights (see diagram, page 134, for placement). Cut a panel of lattice to size. Tack the lattice panel to the inner surfaces of the outer trim strips. Then secure it by sandwiching it between the outer trim strips and the inner strips and driving 1½-inch deck screws through the inner strips and lattice and into the outer strips. See illustration for details. Set a pair of 24-inch-wide plastic window box planters into the box for planting.

Cutting Lattice Panels

Lattice panels are quick and easy to use, but they typically are made with relatively flimsy strips of thin wood held together with staples, which leaves them a bit fragile. To cut a lattice panel to size without the saw vibration causing the panels to break apart, clamp the panel between two thin strips of scrap wood before cutting it, and then cut through the scraps and the lattice at the same time.

DOG BONE PET BED

When it comes to spoiling your faithful canine, there is no such thing as too cute

If you're creating that perfect little getaway in your own backyard, why not include a nice place for your pet as well? Dogs give so much and ask little in return. Creating a place for your dog that's comfortable is a great addition to your deck or patio.

A pet bed is an easy project that can be completed in a day, and you can get creative with additions to the basic design. A roof to protect from rain and sun, or built-ins like water or food bowls are easy upgrades.

It's a good idea to adjust the dimensions in this project to suit your dog. Be sure it's strong enough, and add framing to support your pet's size and weight, if needed. The bed featured here was built to support the weight of a 10- to 20-pound dog. Two-by lumber should be used for larger dogs.

PET BED

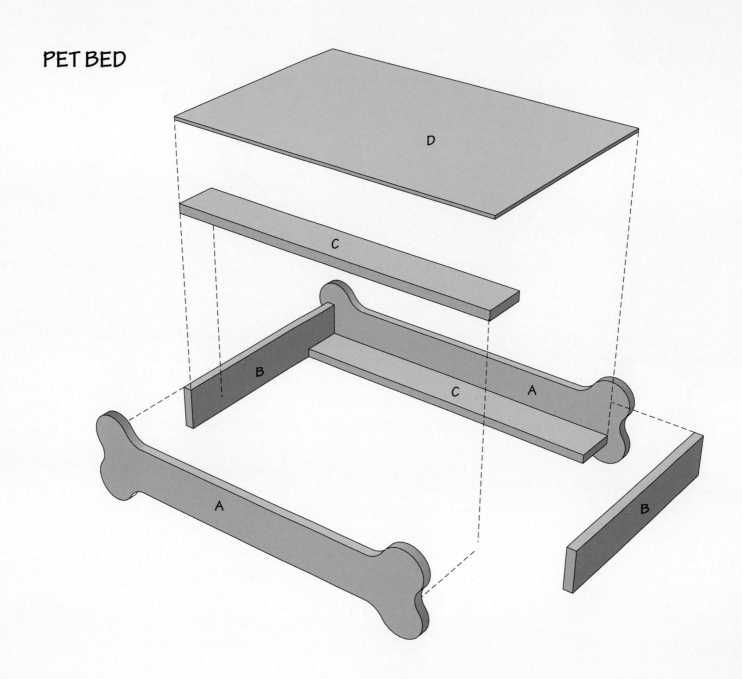

Cutting List

Key	Qty	Description	Size
A	2	Box Front/Back	¾ x 7¼ x 30 in.
B	2	Box Sides	¾ x 3½ x 18 in.
C	2	Bed Supports	¾ x 3½ x 27 in.
D	1	Bed Board	¼ x 18 x 27 in.

Materials List

Qty	Description	Tools	
	(Pine)	Drill/driver	Circular saw
1	1 x 8 in. x 8 ft.	Pocket hole jig	Jigsaw
1	1 x 4 in. x 8 ft.	Tape measure	Clamps
	24 x 48 in. ¼-in. plywood	Square	
	1¼-in. pocket screws		
	1½-in. deck screws		
	¾-in. deck screws		
	Glue		
	Sealer or exterior gloss paint		

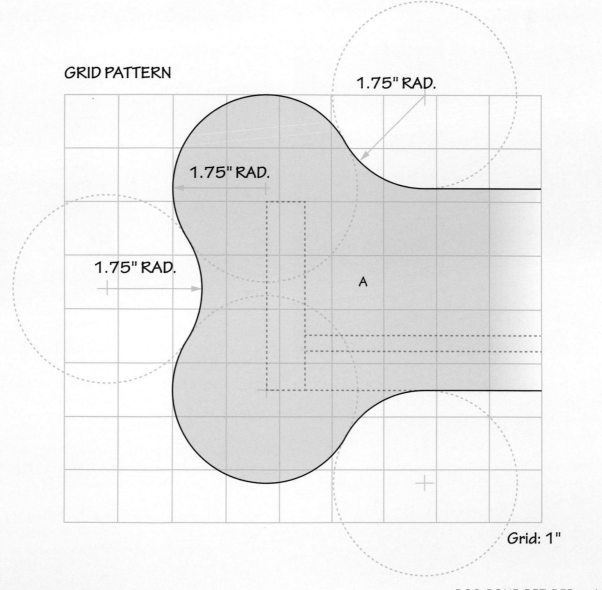

GRID PATTERN

1.75" RAD.

1.75" RAD.

1.75" RAD.

A

Grid: 1"

How to Build a Dog Bone Pet Bed

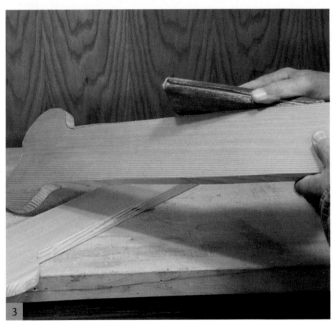

(#1) The bone-shaped panels for the bed box are cut from 1 x 8 cedar. Lay out the shapes directly onto the 1 x 8 using a compass, tape measure, and straightedge. See page 141 for the layout plan.

> **TIP:** Lay out, cut, and sand one side and then use it as a template for drawing the shape for the second panel to ensure uniform results.

(#2) Securely clamp the workpiece to your worksurface and carefully cut the profiles with a jigsaw. Cut slightly outside the cutting lines so you can sand them back right to the line.

(#3) Sand the curved shapes and ease any sharp edges on the workpiece. Use a sanding block or a couple of power sanders (a random orbit sander and a detail sander would work).

(#4) Cut the rectangular side pieces for the bed box and prepare to join them to the bone-shaped panels. We used pocket screws to make clean, strong joints (see page 15).

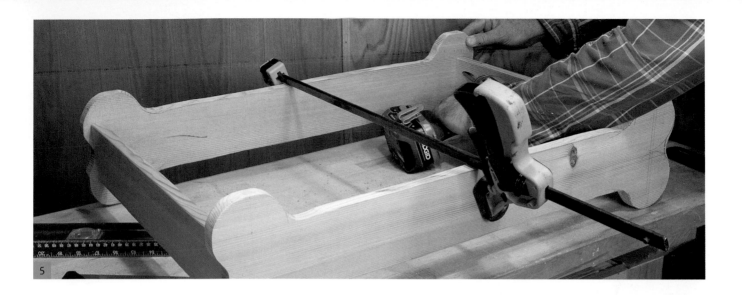

(#5) Clamp the box panels together and join them with glue and screws. If you prefer, you could glue the joints and reinforce them by driving 8d casing nails through the front and back and into the ends of the side pieces. Then drive additional nails through the box and into the bed supports (step 6) on all sides.

(#6) Attach the bed supports between the front and back panels. The supports should be flush with the bottom edges of the box panels (exclusive of the bone shapes). If you are nailing the joints, drive a few 8d casing nails through the box and into all three butting edges of each bed support.

(#7) Cut the bed board to size from ¼-inch-thick exterior rated plywood. Attach it by driving ¾-deck screws through the bed board and into the bed supports. Apply your desired finish, such as a clear wood sealer with UV protection or exterior paint (gloss is best). For sanitation and ease of cleaning, paint the bed board on the top and the underside with a glossy exterior paint. Purchase or make a pet bed "mattress" and place it into the bed.

CONCRETE CANDLE HOLDERS

These three tabletop tea-light holders illuminate the sophisticated beauty of cast concrete

F ew environmental elements can beat candlelight when it comes to setting the mood. The effect is even more intensified when the candlelight is emanating from an elegant handmade candleholder. These tea light holders can be constructed and built in a matter of hours but will shine on for years, adding that perfect ambiance to your deck or patio.

Don't be intimidated by using concrete. It does not have to mean lugging heavy bags of cement, sand, and rock and expending a lot of energy. Concrete mixes take the work out of figuring out a proper recipe, and with the small size of this project, the amounts you mix will be light enough to keep from straining any muscles.

CANDLE HOLDERS

CANDLE HOLDER A

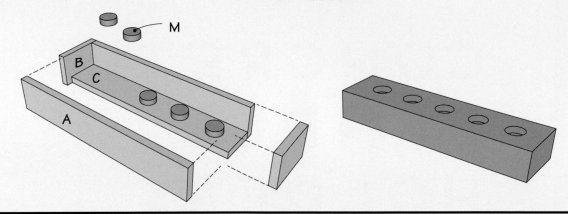

CANDLE HOLDER B

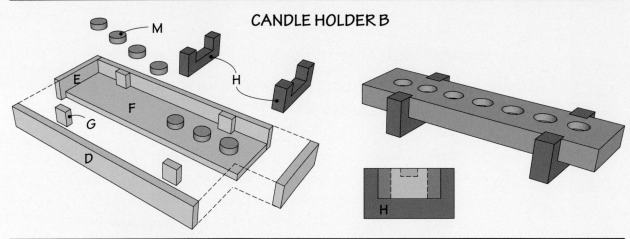

CANDLE HOLDER C

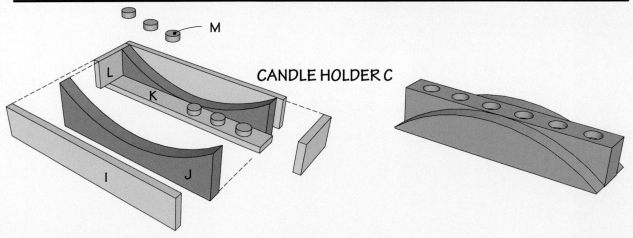

Cutting List

CANDLE HOLDER A (Overall Size: 1¾ x 3½ x 14 in.)

Key	Qty	Description	Size
A	2	Side Forms	¾ x 2½ x 14 in.
B	2	End Forms	¾ x 2½ x 5 in.
C	1	Bottom Form	3½ x 3½ x 14 in.
M	5	Knockouts	

CANDLE HOLDER B (Overall Size: 1¾ x 5½ x 16 in.)

Key	Qty	Description	Size
D	2	Side Forms	¾ x 2½ x 16 in.
E	2	End Forms	¾ x 2½ x 7 in.
F	1	Bottom Form	¾ x 5½ x 16 in.
G	4	Side Channel Forms	1 x 1½ x 1¾ in.
H	2	Wood Stands	1½ x 3½ x 8 in.
M	7	Knockouts	

CANDLE HOLDER C (Overall Size: 3½ x 5½ x 15 in.)

Key	Qty	Description	Size
I	2	Side Forms	¾ x 3½ x 17½ in.
J	2	Inside Forms	1½ x 5½ x 15 in.
K	1	Bottom Form	¾ x 2½ x 17½ in.
L	2	End Forms	¾ x 2½ x 5½ in.
M	6	Knockouts	

Materials List

Qty	Description
	(Pine)
1	1 x 2 in. x 8 ft.
2	1 x 3 in. x 8 ft.
1	1 x 4 in. x 8 ft.
1	1 x 6 in. x 8 ft.
	1¼-in.-dia. PVC pipe (18 in.)
1	60-lb. bag concrete mix
	1½-in. screws
	Silicone caulk
	Masking tape
	Nonstick cooking spray
	Concrete sealer (optional)

Tools
Mixing tub
5-gal. bucket with lid or mortar box
Small tarp or plastic sheeting

Start with a suitable concrete premix. A countertop formula, which is made with finer aggregates, is a good choice. Use a 5-gallon container with a tight-fitting lid to store the concrete. A plastic cup makes a handy scoop and is easy for measuring.

How to Make Concrete Candle Holders (3 Options)

(#1) Build the form or forms from 1 x 2, 1 x 3, and 1 x 5 stock, based on the design used. Any smooth lumber will work, unless you want a rough finish. Mark the locations of the candles on the insides of the forms. Clamp the forms together and check measurements, then drill holes and fasten the forms together with 1½-inch screws.

NOTE: For this project, I built three different casting forms and then cast all three at once.

(#2) For the round spaces, or knockouts, that will hold the candles, use wood dowels or 1¼-inch PVC pipe cut to ¾ inch, then wrap them in masking tape. Make a cut in the plastic pipe ring to make it easier to squeeze and remove once the concrete has cured.

(#3) Use caulk to adhere the candle knockouts into the form. It's sometimes hard to get your head around, but casting concrete is almost always done upside-down, so concentrate and keep your bearings.

(#4) Apply a thin bead of caulk in the corners and any gaps between the wood forms, then wipe or spray the inside of the form with any light oil as a release agent. Nonstick cooking spray works well.

(#5) Measure out enough concrete mix for your form or forms and dump it into a bucket or mortar box. A tarp or plastic sheet over your work area will ease cleanup later. Add water in small amounts and mix well. The mix should be the consistency of sticky oatmeal. With the form on a flat surface, pour or scoop the concrete into the mold, packing it down gently into the corners.

Note: Always wear gloves and a dust mask when mixing or handling concrete.

(#6) Gently tap the sides of the mold several times with a rubber mallet to settle the material, to fill all the voids, and to release air bubbles. For most forms, fill with concrete mix to the top and strike off any excess by dragging a piece of scrap wood across the top in a sawing motion. Cover the form with plastic sheeting and let the concrete cure for three to five days.

(#7) Disassemble the form by removing the screws and carefully prying the form away from the dried concrete. Remove the candle knockout.

(#8) The concrete can be sanded and polished with a diamond sanding pad, a sanding block and regular sandpaper, or emery paper. Concrete stain may also be used to change the color of the concrete (you can add it to the wet mixture before casting too). Sealing the concrete after three or four weeks will add protection from the elements and will deepen the color.

23

FIRE BOWL

Cast a relaxing glow on your outdoor entertaining and gaze at the dancing flames as long as you wish

Fire pits, chimneys, and outdoor fireplaces are incredibly popular. They offer warmth, light, and ambiance that many enjoy. But the smoke, soot, and smell they produce is often a nuisance, and some cities and towns have begun passing ordinances limiting backyard fires.

This fire bowl project offers a great solution. It's small enough to use just about anywhere, large enough to provide light and heat, and produces no smoke or smell. Its simple shape is appealing and uses about half of a 60-pound bag of concrete mix, making it light enough to move when needed. Lava rock is used as an infill around cans of gel fuel (available in low-carbon-monoxide formulations for indoor use). They provide a safe way to hold the fuel in place and are nearly impervious to the heat generated by the fire. The cans of gel fuel can be lit and extinguished easily.

A liquid color agent can be added to the concrete mix, giving the vessel another level of visual excitement. Leaves, decorative rocks, and tiles can be added to the exterior mold before pouring to personalize the finished product.

As with any fire, never leave it unattended, and be sure it is out when you're finished enjoying its warmth and light.

FIRE BOWL

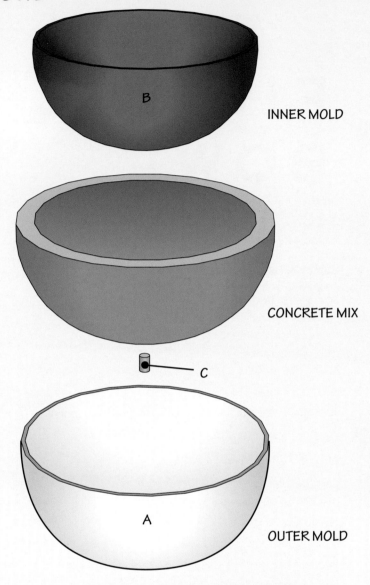

INNER MOLD

CONCRETE MIX

C

OUTER MOLD

Fire Bowl Mold

Key	Qty	Description	Size
A	1	Outer Mold	18-in. dia.
B	1	Inner Mold	16 -in. dia.
C	1	Dowel or Cork	½-in. dia. x 1½ in.

Materials List

Qty	Description	Tools
1	18–20-in. bowl	Bricks or stones for weight
1	16–18-in. bowl	Mortar box
1	60-lb. bag concrete mix	Small tarp or plastic sheeting
	Lava rock	Screwdriver
	Gel fuel	Tile file
	Nonstick cooking spray	
	Liquid concrete color (optional)	

How to Cast a Concrete Fire Bowl

(#1) The most important part of building the fire bowl is finding the right molds (plastic bowls). Two will be needed. First, there's the inner mold, which displaces the concrete; then an outer mold holds the concrete and creates the shape of the fire bowl. The molds shown are a plastic punch bowl and planter. Be sure they are sturdy enough to hold wet concrete, and spray them with a release agent before filling. A dowel or cork is glued to the bottom of the inner mold to keep it from sinking too far into the mix and to create a drainage hole once the concrete has dried.

(#2) Mix the concrete following the manufacturer's instructions.

(#3) Pour the concrete mixture into the outer mold, gently pushing it around the bottom evenly. Bounce the bowl on your worksurface lightly to help the concrete settle.

TIP: A darker colored concrete has an elegance that comes from the fact that its tone does not look like a sidewalk or driveway. Add liquid concrete color (black) when mixing the concrete. Be aware that it takes a lot. A one-pint bottle will alter the "sidewalk gray" color to a darker gray.

(#4) Press the inner mold into the concrete, then continue adding concrete, gently pushing it into the sides between the inner and outer molds. Add bricks or stones to the inner mold to keep it from floating above the concrete as it dries (and float it will).

(#5) Add more stones to the inner mold to make sure it stays in place. Use a stick to gently move the concrete down between the molds. Cover with plastic and let the concrete dry for at least two or three days.

(#6) Pry the inner mold from the concrete with a screwdriver and then carefully turn the bowl over to remove the concrete bowl from the outer mold.

(#7) Clean up your casting. A diamond tile file will take out any imperfections on the top and corners.

(#8) Place a brick or tile in the bottom of the bowl, then set the gel fuel can or cans (this fire bowl easily accommodates three cans) on top. Add lava rock, carefully locking the cans into the bowl's center.

VARIATION: Make the Flames Dance

Most of us love to sit and watch flames. By stocking your fire bowl with three cans of gel fuel surrounded by lava rock, flames are what you'll get (don't expect a bonfire; it's a bit subtler than that).

Here is another way you can enjoy your fire bowl: make it exactly as is described on the previous pages. Then pick up a round grill grate from a kettle-style charcoal grill (the grate that supports the coals, not the one you cook on). Cut some expanded metal mesh to the same size and shape as the grate. Cut a couple small notches in the mesh on opposite sides so you can get at the grate with pliers.

Then visit your local craft supply store and pick up a couple of bags of fire-rated colored glass beads. After you've arranged your gel fuel cans in the bowl, place the grate and mesh over the cans and then scatter the colored beads atop the mesh so you can watch them glow when the gel fuel burns.

Rau+Barber

Rau+Barber

24

INLAID CONCRETE PLANTER

This planter project proves that even concrete can be cute

Nothing says cool industrial chic like furnishings with a little concrete flair. And this cute planter project fills the bill. Plus, it's a relatively easy accessory to create from scratch.

There are several considerations to keep in mind when working with concrete, but perhaps the first (and most important) is weight. While it's one of the most versatile building materials available, its weight can be a drawback. Concrete typically weighs 145 pounds per cubic foot, so design and dimensions are important.

Keeping the planter small is an obvious first step in reducing the weight. Casters can make moving the planter easier. Try to keep whatever you create within a total of 0.6 cubic feet, which is the volume of a typical 80-pound bag of concrete. At 8 x 8 x 11 inches, this planter design is large enough to be useful and have a presence on your deck or patio but still consumes only 0.4 cubic feet of concrete.

Consider adding stones, tiles, metal parts, or shells to the outside of the form, as we've done here.

NOTE: Always wear gloves and a dust mask when working with concrete.

CONCRETE PLANTER

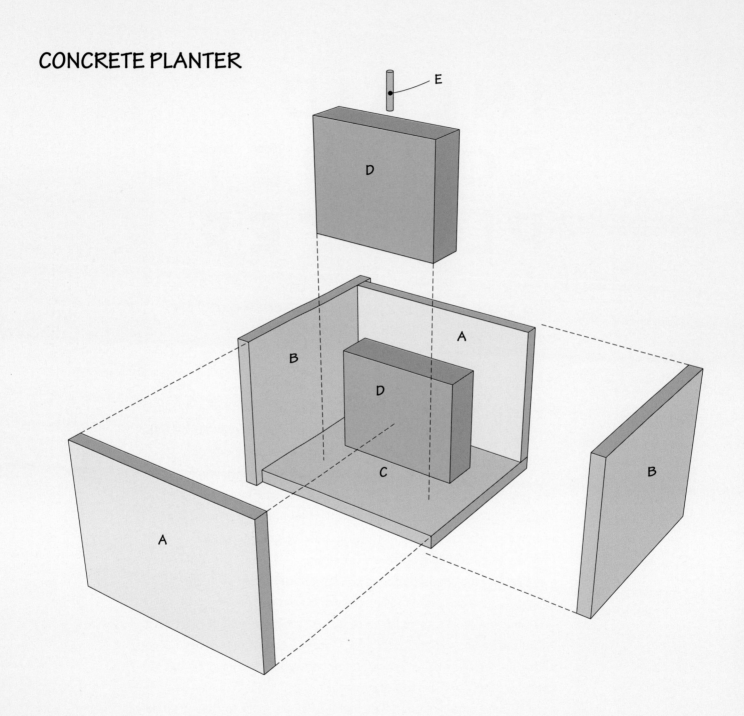

Cutting List

Key	Qty	Description	Size
A	2	Side Forms	¾ x 8 x 11¼ in.
B	2	End Forms	¾ x 8¾ x 11¼ in.
C	1	Base Form	¾ x 9¾ x 11¼ in..
D	2	Foam Knockouts	2 x 6 x 7¼ in.
E	1	Dowel	⅜-in. dia. x 4 in.

Materials List

Qty	Description
1	¾ x 11–¼ x 48 in. melamine shelf
	2-in. rigid foam insulation (2 sq. ft.)
1	60-lb. bag concrete mix
	Masking tape
	1½-in. screws
	2-in. drywall screws
	Silicone caulk
	Coloring agent (optional)

Tools	
Drill/driver	Utility knife or chisel
Mortar box	Small tarp or plastic sheeting
Rubber mallet	

The Hypertufa Option

Gardening magazines and catalogs often feature what appear to be stone or concrete troughs brimming with flowers or planted as alpine gardens. Often, these are made not with concrete but with a material called hypertufa. With hypertufa, you can create inexpensive, long-lasting planters that resemble aged stone sinks or troughs. Because the hypertufa mix uses lightweight soil amendment like perlite or vermiculite instead of heavy stone aggregate, hypertufa is light and manageable. You simply blend up the mix and pour it into a form where it sets up and cures. Hypertufa dries to the color of concrete. If you prefer another color, simply add concrete dye during the mixing process. Tinting products are very concentrated, so start with a small amount and add more if necessary.

A lightweight version of concrete, hypertufa is an easy material to work with and makes beautiful garden accessories.

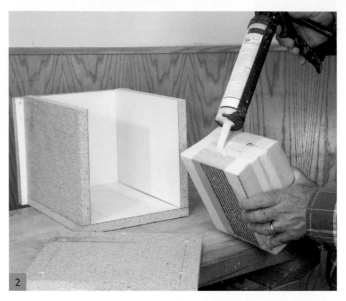

(#1) Build the form using ¾-inch plywood or melamine-coated particleboard. This form was built from one very manageable (and inexpensive) 11¼-wide x 48-inch-long melamine shelf. Start by cutting the base panel and then attach the sides and one of the ends by butting them together and fastening with 1½-inch drywall screws.

(#2) Tape the two blocks of 2-inch rigid foam together to form a knockout for the interior of the planter. Spread an even layer of silicone caulk onto one of the long sides of the foam and then push it securely down onto the base, being sure to keep it centered from side to side. Apply a very thin bead of caulk around the inside edges of the forms.

(#3) Use caulk to stick inserts or inlays to the inside of the form. We attached a small nautilus shell to the form with the more attractive side against the form so it will be visible. Cover the insert with masking tape, then smear a thin coat of caulk across the tape. Push firmly to the inside of the form.

(#4) Mix the concrete according to the manufacturer's instructions. Add a coloring agent if desired. The texture should be roughly that of sticky oatmeal when the concrete is ready.

(#5) Pour the concrete into the mold, working it into the corners. Rap the form gently with a rubber mallet as you fill it to help the concrete settle and to dislodge air bubbles. If you want to add a drain hole (recommended), poke a 6-inch long piece of ⅜- or ½-inch doweling into the center of the foam insert (remember: you're usually working upside down when casting concrete).

(#6) Cover the form with sheet plastic and allow the concrete to dry for three to five days. Then unscrew the panels and gently remove the forms.

(#7) Cut and remove the rigid foam insert using a chisel or utility knife. You will need to break up the foam to get it out, so be prepared for a bit of a mess.

(#8) Clean up the exterior of the planter with a diamond sanding pad, knocking down any ridges or blemishes. Dip the pad in water to prevent generating dust, but do wear a particle mask when doing this. Fill the planter with planting mix and plant your favorite seeds or transplants.

25

CONCRETE BIRDBATH

Modern styling makes this a birdbath that you'll enjoy as much as the birds

Like all animals, birds need water to survive. While they can extract moisture from food, most birds drink water daily. Birds also use water for cleaning. Setting up a birdbath in your yard is a great way to attract birds you won't usually see at your bird feeder. And building your own affords fun and personalization.

This birdbath design is modern, dramatic, and easy to build. It uses a single 80-pound bag of premixed concrete, so it's not difficult to move around your patio. You can add inserts into the concrete for added flair, or use color additives or stain to give it more contrast. A concrete counter top mix is a good choice, as it has smaller aggregates, but any concrete mix will work.

Measure often as you build, adjusting the knockout measurements so that the parts fit together as closely as possible.

CONCRETE BIRDBATH

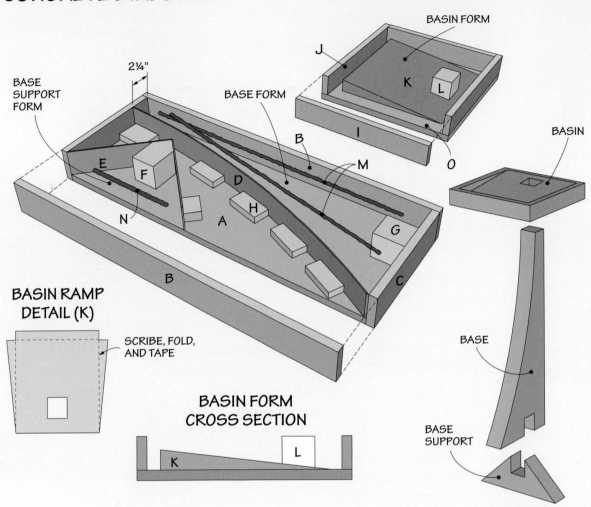

BASE SUPPORT FORM

2¼"

BASE FORM

BASIN FORM

J

K

L

I

O

BASIN

E

F

N

A

D

H

M

B

G

C

B

BASE

BASE SUPPORT

BASIN RAMP DETAIL (K)

SCRIBE, FOLD, AND TAPE

BASIN FORM CROSS SECTION

K

L

KNOCKOUTS DETAIL

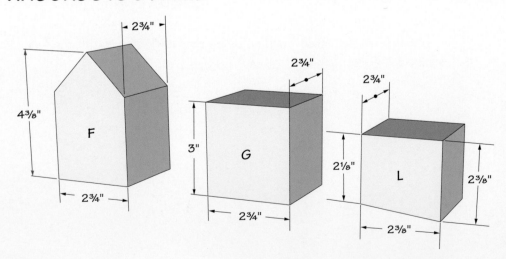

2¾"

4⅜"

F

2¾"

2¾"

3"

G

2¾"

2¾"

2⅛"

L

2⅜"

2⅜"

Cutting List

Key	Qty	Description	Size
A	1	Bottom Mold	¾ x 12 x 33½ in.
B	2	Side Molds	¾ x 3½ x 33½ in.
C	2	End Molds	¾ x 3½ x 12 in.
D	1	Base Arch Mold	⅛ x 2¾ x 35 in.
E	2	Support Angle Molds	⅛ x 2¾ x 10½ in.
F	1	Support Knockout	2¾ x 2¾ x 4⅜ in.
G	1	Base Knockout	2¾ x 2¾ x 3 in.
H	7	Mold Supports	¾ x 1½ x 3 in.
I	2	Basin Side Molds	¾ x 2½ x 12 in.
J	2	Basin End Molds	¾ x 2½ x 13½ in.
K	1	Bottom Basin Knockout	2 x 10 x 10 in.
L	1	Through Basin Knockout	2¾ x 2⅜ x 2⅜ in.
M	2	Rebar	⅜-in. dia. x 30 in.
N	1	Rebar	⅜-in. dia. x 10 in.
O	1	Basin Bottom	12 x 12 in.

Materials List

Qty	Description	Qty	Description
1	1 x 2 in. x 8 ft.	1	80-lb. bag concrete mix
1	1 x 3 in. x 8 ft.		1½-in. screws
1	1 x 4 in. x 8 ft.		2-in. drywall screws
	24 x 48 in. ¾-in. melamine		Silicone caulk
	24 x 48 in. ⅛-in. hardboard		Masking tape
	⅜ in. x 8 ft. rebar		Nonstick cooking spray
	Silicone adhesive		Coloring agent (optional)
	2-in. rigid foam insulation (1 sq. ft.)		

Tools	
Drill/driver	Utility knife
Mixing tub	Small tarp or plastic sheeting

Birdbath Basics

Set up your birdbath in the shade and keep it filled with water at all times. Consider a solar-powered fountain. You can also try hanging a bottle or pail with a tiny hole punched into the bottom over the bath. The slow drip will alert birds that water is nearby, and will keep the basin full of fresh water.

How to Make a Concrete Birdbath

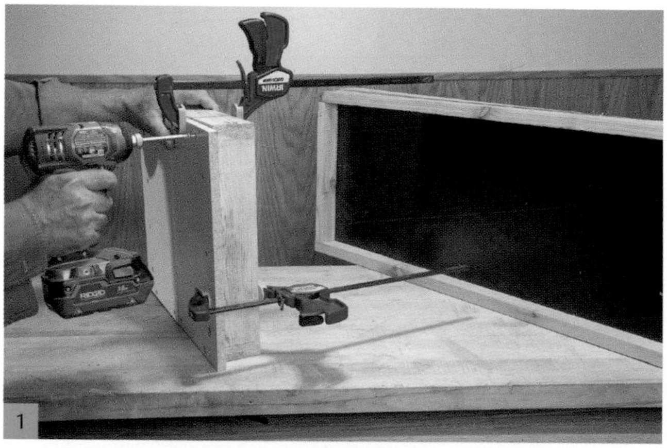

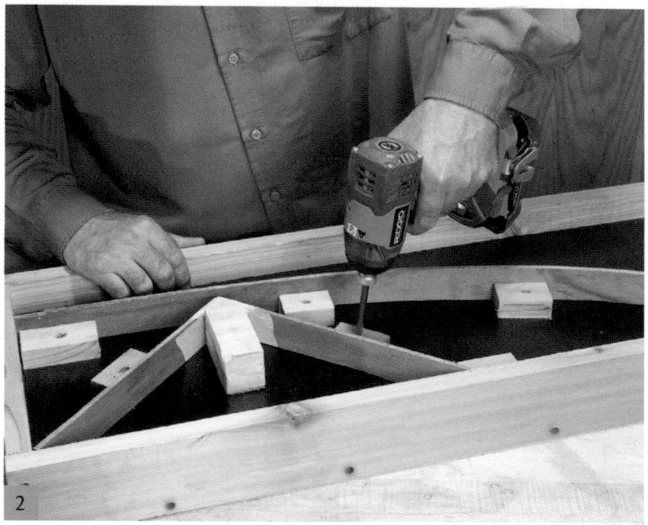

(#1) Build the form boxes for the basin and stand from ¾-inch melamine and 1 x 4 stock, according to the diagram on page 164. Use coarse-thread 1½-inch drywall screws to attach the wood sides to the form boards.

(#2) Create the arched side of the base and support using strips of ⅛-inch hardboard cut into strips that are 2¾ inches wide. Screw blocking cut from scrap to the outside of the hardboard every 6 to 8 inches to hold it in place. Create knockouts at the top and bottom of the base support and base, which will lock the two parts together when complete.

(#3) A form that's 12½ inches square by 2¾ inches deep is used to create the basin. A ramp-shaped insert that's 10 x 10 x 2 inches is applied to the bottom of the form so the bottom of the basin will slope when it is cast. Make the ramp from scrap wood or hardboard taped together.

(#4) Add a knockout made from rigid insulation foam or hardboard to the bottom of the ramp that will allow the base to pass through the back of the bowl. See the illustration on page 164 for details.

(#5) Apply a thin layer of caulk to the bottom edges of the ramp and then press it into the center of the basin.

(#6) Spray the interior surfaces of the molds with nonstick cooking spray as a release agent.

7

8

9

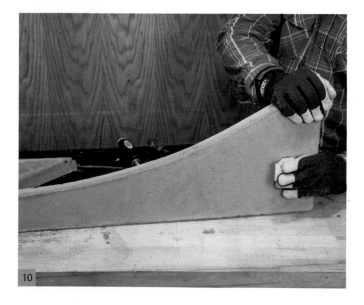

10

(#7) Mix the concrete following the manufacturer's instructions. Add color, aggregates, or inserts, if desired. Pour the concrete mix into the basin and base support molds, spreading it into the corners. Add rebar to the basin support when you have filled the form halfway, and then continue filling the form with concrete.

(#8) Pour concrete mix into the basin mold, making sure the area around the knockout is completely filled in.

(#9) The design of this birdbath is relatively thin, only 1½ inches thick, so let the concrete dry longer and strengthen before attempting to remove the molds—at least four to six days. Then carefully disassemble the molds.

(#10) Remove the knockouts. Cover the concrete pieces with plastic and allow them to cure for another three to four days. Attach the flared feet to opposite sides of the basin support with silicone adhesive. Let the adhesive dry for a couple of days and then fit the basin over the support top.

Metric Conversions

To Convert:	To:	Multiply by:
Inches	Millimeters	25.4
Inches	Centimeters	2.54
Feet	Meters	0.305
Yards	Meters	0.914
Square inches	Square centimeters	6.45
Square feet	Square meters	0.093
Square yards	Square meters	0.836
Ounces	Milliliters	30.0
Pints (U.S.)	Liters	0.473 (Imp. 0.568)
Quarts (U.S.)	Liters	0.946 (Imp. 1.136)
Gallons (U.S.)	Liters	3.785 (Imp. 4.546)
Ounces	Grams	28.4
Pounds	Kilograms	0.454

To Convert:	To:	Multiply by:
Millimeters	Inches	0.039
Centimeters	Inches	0.394
Meters	Feet	3.28
Meters	Yards	1.09
Square centimeters	Square inches	0.155
Square meters	Square feet	10.8
Square meters	Square yards	1.2
Milliliters	Ounces	.033
Liters	Pints (U.S.)	2.114 (Imp. 1.76)
Liters	Quarts (U.S.)	1.057 (Imp. 0.88)
Liters	Gallons (U.S.)	0.264 (Imp. 0.22)
Grams	Ounces	0.035
Kilograms	Pounds	2.2

Converting Temperatures

Convert degrees Fahrenheit (F) to degrees Celsius (C) by following this simple formula: Subtract 32 from the Fahrenheit temperature reading. Then, multiply that number by 5/9. For example, 77°F - 32 = 45. 45 × 5/9 = 25°C.

To convert degrees Celsius to degrees Fahrenheit, multiply the Celsius temperature reading by 9/5. Then, add 32. For example, 25°C × 9/5 = 45. 45 + 32 = 77°F.

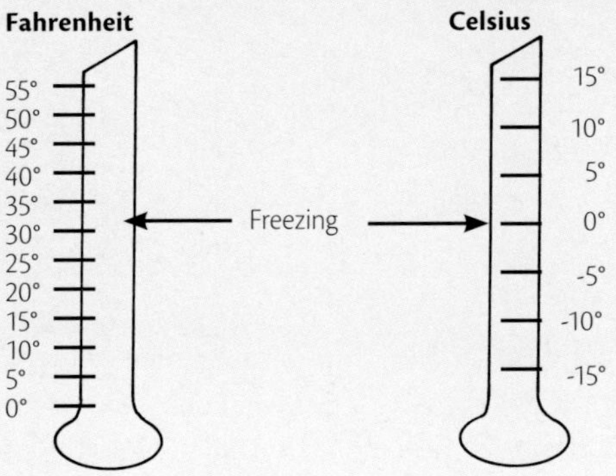

Metric Plywood Panels

Metric plywood panels are commonly available in two sizes: 1,200 mm × 2,400 mm and 1,220 mm × 2,400 mm, which is roughly equivalent to a 4 × 8-ft. sheet. Standard and Select sheathing panels come in standard thicknesses, while Sanded grade panels are available in special thicknesses.

Standard Sheathing Grade		Sanded Grade	
7.5 mm	(5/16 in.)	6 mm	(4/17 in.)
9.5 mm	(3/8 in.)	8 mm	(5/16 in.)
12.5 mm	(1/2 in.)	11 mm	(7/16 in.)
15.5 mm	(5/8 in.)	14 mm	(9/16 in.)
18.5 mm	(3/4 in.)	17 mm	(2/3 in.)
20.5 mm	(13/16 in.)	19 mm	(3/4 in.)
22.5 mm	(7/8 in.)	21 mm	(13/16 in.)
25.5 mm	(1 in.)	24 mm	(15/16 in.)

Lumber Dimensions

Nominal - U.S.	Actual - U.S. (in inches)	Metric
1 × 2	¾ × 1½	19 × 38 mm
1 × 3	¾ × 2½	19 × 64 mm
1 × 4	¾ × 3½	19 × 89 mm
1 × 5	¾ × 4½	19 × 114 mm
1 × 6	¾ × 5½	19 × 140 mm
1 × 7	¾ × 6¼	19 × 159 mm
1 × 8	¾ × 7¼	19 × 184 mm
1 × 10	¾ × 9¼	19 × 235 mm
1 × 12	¾ × 11¼	19 × 286 mm
1¼ × 4	1 × 3½	25 × 89 mm
1¼ × 6	1 × 5½	25 × 140 mm
1¼ × 8	1 × 7¼	25 × 184 mm
1¼ × 10	1 × 9¼	25 × 235 mm
1¼ × 12	1 × 11¼	25 × 286 mm
1½ × 4	1¼ × 3½	32 × 89 mm
1½ × 6	1¼ × 5½	32 × 140 mm
1½ × 8	1¼ × 7¼	32 × 184 mm
1½ × 10	1¼ × 9¼	32 × 235 mm
1½ × 12	1¼ × 11¼	32 × 286 mm
2 × 4	1½ × 3½	38 × 89 mm
2 × 6	1½ × 5½	38 × 140 mm
2 × 8	1½ × 7¼	38 × 184 mm
2 × 10	1½ × 9¼	38 × 235 mm
2 × 12	1½ × 11¼	38 × 286 mm
3 × 6	2½ × 5½	64 × 140 mm
4 × 4	3½ × 3½	89 × 89 mm
4 × 6	3½ × 5½	89 × 140 mm

Liquid Measurement Equivalents

1 Pint	= 16 Fluid Ounces	= 2 Cups
1 Quart	= 32 Fluid Ounces	= 2 Pints
1 Gallon	= 128 Fluid Ounces	= 4 Quarts

Drill Bit Guide

Twist Bit	Self-piloting	Spade Bit	Adjustable Counterbore	Hole Saw
	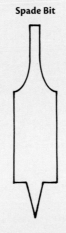	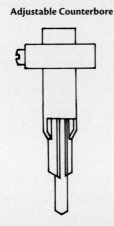	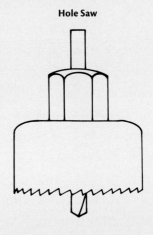	

Counterbore, Shank & Pilot Hole Diameters

Screw Size	Counterbore Diameter for Screw Head	Clearance Hole for Screw Shank	Pilot Hole Diameter	
			Hard Wood	Soft Wood
#1	.146 $^9/_{64}$	$^5/_{64}$	$^3/_{64}$	$^1/_{32}$
#2	¼	$^3/_{32}$	$^3/_{64}$	$^1/_{32}$
#3	¼	$^7/_{64}$	$^1/_{16}$	$^3/_{64}$
#4	¼	⅛	$^1/_{16}$	$^3/_{64}$
#5	¼	$^9/_{64}$	$^5/_{64}$	$^1/_{16}$
#6	$^5/_{16}$	$^5/_{32}$	$^3/_{32}$	$^5/_{64}$
#7	$^5/_{16}$	$^5/_{32}$	$^3/_{32}$	$^5/_{64}$
#8	⅜	$^{11}/_{64}$	⅛	$^3/_{32}$
#9	⅜	$^{11}/_{64}$	⅛	$^3/_{32}$
#10	⅜	$^3/_{16}$	⅛	$^7/_{64}$
#11	½	$^3/_{16}$	$^5/_{32}$	$^9/_{64}$
#12	½	$^7/_{32}$	$^9/_{64}$	⅛

Abrasive Paper Grits - (Aluminum Oxide)

Very Coarse	Coarse	Medium	Fine	Very Fine
12–36	40–60	80–120	150–180	220–600

Selecting the Right Lumber for a Project

Picking the right wood for a project is a decision that will affect the durability and attractiveness of the final product. Some woods are more prone to warping than others, some are more resistant to decay, and some are superior when it comes to accepting a coat of paint. Matching styles and wood varieties will help to create a common theme throughout your home.

Lumber sizes such as 2 × 4 are nominal dimensions, not actual dimensions. The actual size of lumber is slightly smaller than the nominal size. When it is originally milled, lumber is cut at the nominal size; however, the boards are then planed down for a smoother finish, producing the actual dimensions you buy in the store. See the chart on the opposite page for nominal and actual dimensions.

Softwood	Description	Uses
Cedar	Easy to cut, holds paint well. Heartwood resists decay.	Decks, shakes, shingles, posts, and other decay-prone surfaces.
Fir, larch	Stiff, hard wood. Holds nails well. Some varieties are hard to cut.	Framing materials, flooring, and subflooring.
Pine	Lightweight, soft wood with a tendency to shrink. Holds nails well. Some varieties resist decay.	Paneling, trim, siding, and decks.
Redwood	Lightweight, soft wood that holds paint well. Easy to cut. Heartwood resists decay and insect damage.	Outdoor applications, such as decks, posts, and fences.
Treated lumber	Chemically treated to resist decay. Use corrosion-resistant fasteners only. Wear protective eye wear and clothing to avoid skin, lung, and eye irritation.	Ground-contact and other outdoor applications where resistance to decay is important.

Hardwood	Description	Uses
Birch	Hard, strong wood that is easy to cut and holds paint well.	Painted cabinets, trim, and plywood.
Maple	Heavy, hard, strong wood that is difficult to cut with hand tools.	Flooring, furniture, and countertops.
Poplar	Soft, light wood that is easy to cut with hand or power tools.	Painted cabinets, trim, tongue-and-groove paneling, and plywood cores.
Oak	Heavy, hard, strong wood that is difficult to cut with hand tools.	Furniture, flooring, doors, and trim.
Walnut	Heavy, hard, strong wood that is easy to cut.	Fine woodwork, paneling, and mantelpieces.

Type	Description	Common Nominal Sizes	Actual Sizes
Dimensional lumber 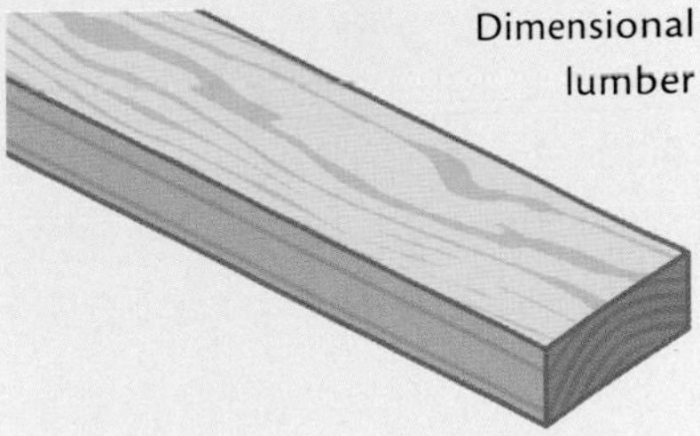	Used in framing of walls, ceilings, floors, and rafters, structural finishing, exterior decking, fencing, and stairs.	1 × 4 1 × 6 1 × 8 2 × 2 2 × 4 2 × 6 2 × 8	¾" × 3½" ¾" × 5½" ¾" × 7¼" 1½" × 1½" 1½" × 3½" 1½" × 5½" 1½" × 7¼"
Furring strips 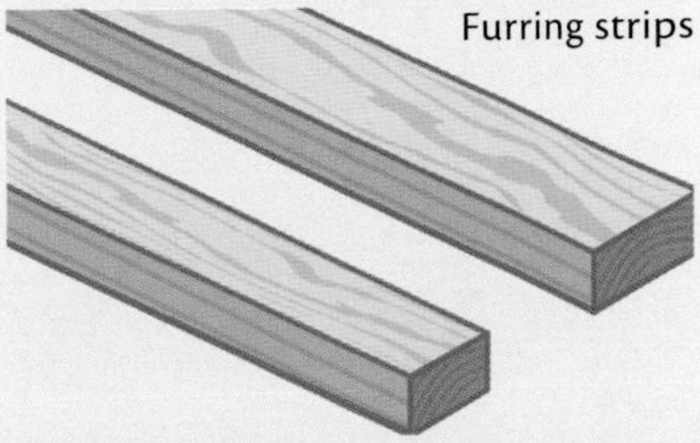	Used in framing of walls, ceilings, floors, and rafters, structural finishing, exterior decking, fencing, and stairs.	1 × 2 1 × 3	¾" × 1½" ¾" × 2½"
Tongue-and-groove paneling 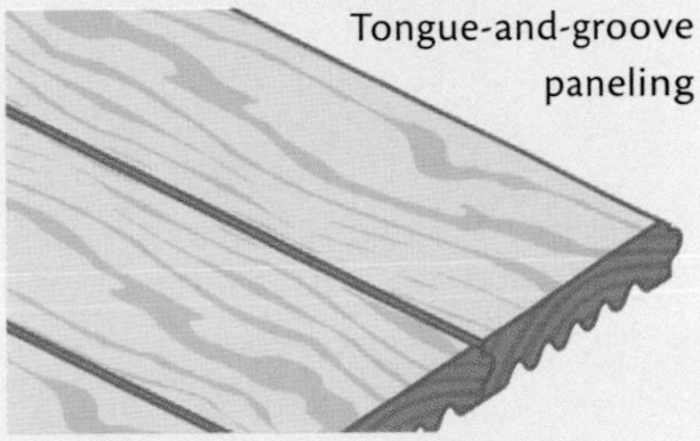	Used in wainscoting and full-length paneling of walls and ceilings.	5⁄16" × 4 1 × 4 1 × 6 1 × 8	Varies, depending on milling process and application.
Finished boards 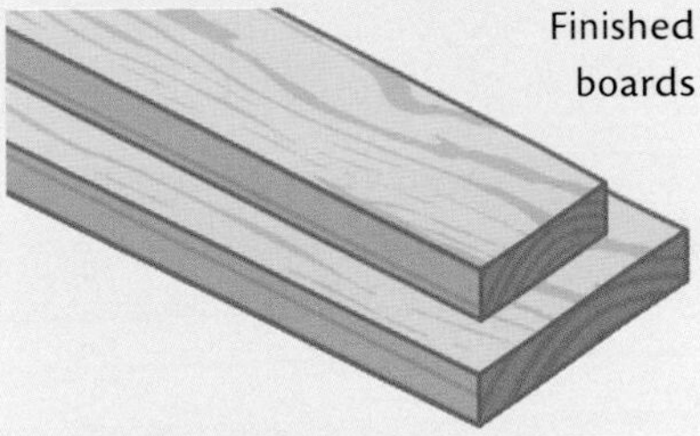	Used in trim, shelving, cabinetry, and other applications where a fine finish is required.	1 × 4 1 × 6 1 × 8 1 × 10 1 × 12	¾" × 3½" ¾" × 5½" ¾" × 7½" ¾" × 9½" ¾" × 11½"
Glue laminate 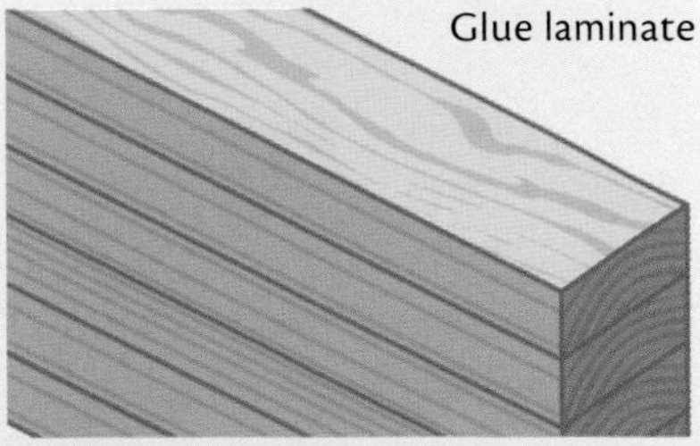	Composed of layers of lumber laminated to form a solid piece. Used for beams and joists.	4 × 10 4 × 12 6 × 10 6 × 12	3½" × 9" 3½" × 12" 3½" × 9" 3½" × 12"
Micro-lam 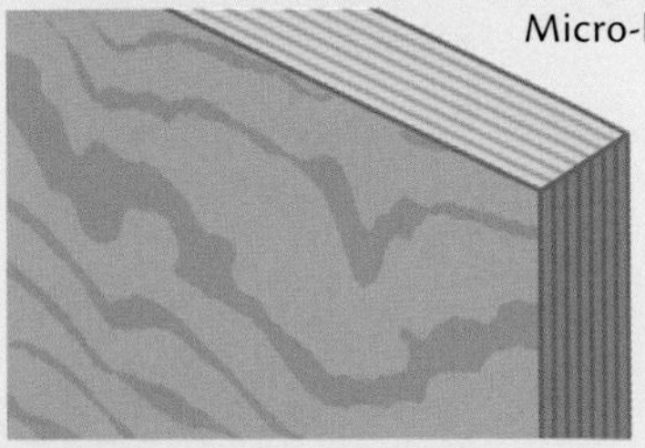	Composed of thin layers glued together for use in joists and beams.	4 × 12	3½" × 11⅜"

Lumber Grading Chart

Grade stamps provide valuable information about a piece of lumber. The lumber's grade is usually indicated by the largest number stamped on the wood. Also stamped on each piece of lumber are its moisture content, species, and lumber mill of origin.

Grade	Description, uses
Clear	Free of knots and defects.
SEL STR or Select Structural	Good appearance, strength, and stiffness.
1,2,3	1,2,3 grades indicate knot size.
CONST or Construction	Both grades used for general framing.
STAND or Standard	Good strength and serviceability.
STUD or Stud	Special designation used in any stud application, including load-bearing walls.
UTIL or Utility	Economical choice for blocking and bracing.

Much of today's lumber is still fairly wet when it is sold, so it's hard to predict how it will behave as it dries. But a quick inspection of each board at the lumberyard or home center will help you disqualify flawed boards. Lumber that is cupped, twisted, or crooked should not be used at full length. However, you may be able to cut out good sections for use as blocking or other short framing pieces. If a board is slightly bowed, you can probably flatten it out as you nail it. Checks, wanes, and knots are cosmetic flaws that seldom affect the strength of the board. The exception is a knot that is loose or missing. In this case, cut off the damaged area. Sections with splits should also be cut off. Splits are likely to spread as the wood dries.

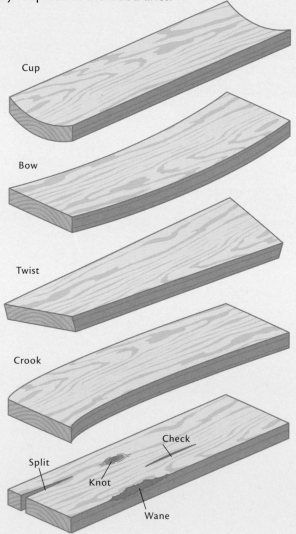

INDEX

MEET THE AUTHOR

Michael R. Anderson has worked as a graphic designer, illustrator, photographer, and writer in both advertising and editorial positions. He served as art director for *HANDY* magazine, where he designed several home-improvement projects, for over 10 years. He presently works as a technical illustrator in Minneapolis, Minnesota.

MEET THE AUTHOR

Michael R. Anderson has worked as a graphic designer, illustrator, photographer, and writer in both advertising and editorial positions. He served as art director for *HANDY* magazine, where he designed several home-improvement projects, for over 10 years. He presently works as a technical illustrator in Minneapolis, Minnesota.

Outdoor Kitchens & Fireplaces

Tina Skinner

$\mathscr{A}$cknowledgements

Dinah Roseberry, Editor and Copywriter
Ginger Doyle, Photo Editor
Anna Carpenter & Julie Smith Taylor, Lifestyle Advisors
Craig Sibol, Fire Master

Copyright © 2008 by Schiffer Publishing, Ltd.
Library of Congress Control Number: 2007942544

Type set in Bernhard Modern BT/New Bskvll BT

ISBN: 978-0-7643-2955-5
Printed in China

Cover photos courtesy of Mid Continent Cabinetry, Paragon Pools, Joyce Hoshall Interiors, Green Scene Landscape, Green Planet Landscaping, and Town and Country Cedar Homes

Schiffer Books are available at special discounts for bulk purchases for sales promotions or premiums. Special editions, including personalized covers, corporate imprints, and excerpts can be created in large quantities for special needs. For more information contact the publisher:

Published by Schiffer Publishing Ltd.
4880 Lower Valley Road
Atglen, PA 19310
Phone: (610) 593-1777; Fax: (610) 593-2002
E-mail: Info@schifferbooks.com

For the largest selection of fine reference books on this and related subjects, please visit our
web site at
www.schifferbooks.com
We are always looking for people to write books on new and related subjects. If you have an idea for a book please contact us at the above address.

This book may be purchased from the publisher.
Include $3.95 for shipping.
Please try your bookstore first.
You may write for a free catalog.

In Europe, Schiffer books are distributed by
Bushwood Books
6 Marksbury Ave.
Kew Gardens
Surrey TW9 4JF England
Phone: 44 (0) 20 8392-8585; Fax: 44 (0) 20 8392-9876
E-mail: info@bushwoodbooks.co.uk
Website: www.bushwoodbooks.co.uk
Free postage in the U.K., Europe; air mail at cost.

Contents

Introduction

Financial analysts keep coming back with more good news for the home improvement industry, as homeowners continue to feather their nests and improve their domestic lifestyles. One of the hottest trends is taking place behind the home, where backyards are being transformed into paradises. Patios and pools are being overshadowed by the addition of outdoor cooking appliances and fireplaces, creating kitchens and living rooms in the open air.

Cooking outside is hardly a new concept. The grill has long been the centerpiece of any outdoor activity, and even our ancestors recognized the utility of cooking outside when it's hot, keeping the heat out of the home itself. Today's trend, however, is toward glamour, comfort, and convenience. Running water, refrigeration, and full ranges are among the amenities being planned into the kitchen out back. Wood-fired ovens make for memorable pizza parties, and extended countertops create a restaurant-like experience, without "dining out." To digest all this open-air cuisine, backyard living rooms include comfy, upholstered furnishings and fireplaces that mesmerize and banish the chill.

This book takes you into more than 100 backyards where you can explore the clever ways in which indoor living has been brought outdoors. The focus is on fire, be it in a built-in barbecue grill, wood-fired oven, fire pit, or towering fireplace. However, you'll also see all the furnishings and accouterments of fine living, as well as the architecture of escaping outside, whether a pergola or pavilion, an extended roofline, or a sunken patio with built-in seating. You'll find hundreds of ideas for furnishing your own backyard. You might never want to step inside your house again!

Grill Centers

The outdoor kitchen is an outgrowth of the barbecue. From hibachi to propane, the grill has long been a fixture of the American lifestyle. Here is the grill on steroids. Stainless steel grill units are finding themselves at home in permanent backyard islands of stone and brick, surrounded by smooth countertops perfect for food preparation and buffet-style serving. Though you'll find a barbecue unit in nearly every back yard featured in this book, this chapter focuses on these altars to the art of barbecue.

A built-in grill sits shrine-like within a tile and stone alcove.
Courtesy of Green Planet Landscaping

Photography by Snap It

Stainless steel caps countertop and backsplash, and the metal work continues above and beyond in a playful expression of the artistry of cooking that takes place below.
Courtesy of Patio Pools & Spas

5

Tropical landscaping makes this setting lush and inviting. *Courtesy of Green Planet Landscaping*

Photography by Keith Frederick, Environmental Landscape Associates Inc.

A slash of half wall houses outdoor kitchen appliances and forms a table at the end for dining. *Courtesy of Environmental Landscape Associates Inc.*

A custom kitchen unit incorporates contemporary steel appliances set in an angular surround and countertop. *Courtesy of Patio Pools & Spas*

A modern and functional cooking area is but a simple extension of the home. *Courtesy of Patio Pools & Spas*

Courtesy of Green Scene Landscape

This outdoor kitchen features a split-level concrete counter-top, inlaid with colored glass and ground to a smooth finish.
Courtesy of Green Scene Landscape

A brick surround forms a timeless backdrop for the latest in outdoor grilling technology. *Courtesy Joyce Hoshall Interiors*

A family utilizes their entire backyard, with seat walls and separate living spaces forming a "floor plan" for the outdoor rooms. *Courtesy of Green Scene Landscape*

The sun may overlook this little grill station day and night, but it's after the lights dim that the fiber optic countertop glass chips shine forth. *Courtesy of Green Scene Landscape*

Ultra modern and convenient, even storm clouds won't keep the chef indoors with this fine kitchen. *Courtesy of Green Scene Landscape*

A pretty tile backsplash defines the space for the outdoor kitchen within a meticulously landscaped backyard environment. *Courtesy of Green Scene Landscape*

An outdoor kitchen includes an incomparable view of the lush woodlands. *Courtesy of Realm Designs, Inc.*   *Photography by Morris Gindi*

This Spanish influenced outdoor kitchen and patio is conveniently located right off the back patio doors, making food preparation easy. Take three steps up to the nearby dining area or lounge by the pool. *Courtesy of Sundancer Creations*

Cheerful colors and sunshine enhance this outdoor kitchen and dining area, tucked under an overhang. *Courtesy of Sundancer Creations*

Here's the ultimate in local "bar and grill," located poolside.
Courtesy of Green Planet Landscaping

Tile and stucco add classic Southwestern appeal to an outdoor kitchen. *Courtesy of Green Planet Landscaping*

A small backyard is no big challenge when designing an outdoor kitchen. The space seems enlarged with the addition of elevated lounging spaces and the avoidance of straight lines. *Courtesy of Green Planet Landscaping*

An elevated cooking area with crisp stainless steel appliances and a multi-color backsplash gives a modern feel to an inviting backyard. *Courtesy of Green Planet Landscaping*

Kiln-melted/fired till flat, wine bottles find a new life as decorative elements in an outdoor kitchen, embedded in a circular concrete countertop and tiled to a backsplash behind the barbecue unit. The wide shot shows the themed outdoor kitchen before the backsplash was completed. *Courtesy of Green Scene Landscape*

Wood-fired Ovens

In a return to ancestral cooking, the wood-fired oven is re-emerging as an upscale outdoor kitchen must-have. Fired quick with small pieces of wood, the fire is brushed to the sides and back, and a pizza or amazing loaf of bread is produced very quickly in the hot oven. Besides producing food that tastes incredible, wood-fired ovens are often lovely sculptural additions to the backyard.

Brick and stucco form a beautiful marriage in this outdoor kitchen setting, the centerpiece of which is a wood-fired oven crowned by a red tile roof. *Courtesy of Los Angeles Ovenworks*

This outdoor area has both a wood-fired oven and a full fireplace finished in flagstone. *Courtesy of Los Angeles Ovenworks*

A beehive unit is home to a fireplace and wood-fired oven in old-fashioned Southwestern style, while nearby a pergola overlooks an outdoor kitchen outfitted with the latest in stainless steel appliances. *Courtesy of Los Angeles Ovenworks*

River stone creates a colorful finish for a cookcenter with a grill and wood-fired oven. *Courtesy of Los Angeles Ovenworks*

Wood-fired ovens are the ideal choice for cooking out of doors, and the varied construction can flatter any outdoor room design. *Courtesy of Los Angeles Ovenworks*

Backyard Bars

Whether indulging in iced teas or alcoholic beverages, the backyard bar acts as a magnet. Just like the noisy inside places where people pay to gather around a bar, the backyard bar creates a place to congregate. In this case, however, drinks are on the house, and service always comes with a smile.

Bar seating adds elevation and elation to a gathering.
Courtesy of Green Planet Landscaping

The recycled bottle motif of this outdoor kitchen preparation/serving area employs dazzling light effects to enhance nighttime entertaining, while providing a bottle and cut-glass design that is pleasing in the daylight hours as well.
Courtesy of Green Scene Landscape

Another countertop with bottle and champagne glass insets adds fun to a poolside kitchen. *Courtesy of Green Scene Landscape*

River stone and Craftsman-style woodwork creates an exciting backyard bar and counter. *Courtesy of Green Scene Landscape*

Bar stools provide an observation perch for spectators to watch the grill chef in action. *Courtesy of Green Scene Landscape*

A split-level concrete countertop with tile accents provides one level for food preparation and another for enjoying it. *Courtesy of Green Scene Landscape*

Three barstools sit close to the cook's inner sanctum, where a built-in beverage center sits flush with the countertop and a condiment tray makes garnishing cocktails a quick task. *Courtesy of Green Scene Landscape*

A fireplace and built-in bar both offer comfort on a cool evening. *Courtesy of Green Planet Landscaping*

Tile tops an expansive countertop encircling a compact outdoor kitchen, advantageously positions poolside. *Courtesy of Green Planet Landscaping*

Dining Outdoors

The picnic table has made way for fancier furnishings in today's upscale backyards. Upholstery fabrics engineered for the outdoors add comfort to a multi-course meal. Anyone planning on cooking outdoors will want to provide seating in which to enjoy the fruits of their labor. Here is a sampling of outdoor dining rooms.

A big, rustic plank table and a brick fireplace take friends and family back in time when they gather below this spacious overhang. *Courtesy of Sundancer Creations*

Two tables and an enormous pergola accommodate a crowd for lunch or dinner. *Courtesy of Sundancer Creations*

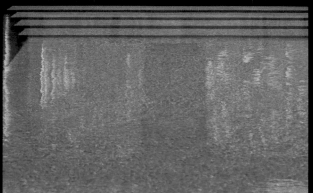

Curtains invoke instant privacy, and firelight the romantic inspiration. *Courtesy Conrad Imports, Inc.*

Though close to the neighboring home, this scene feels enclosed and in touch with nature—a pure habitat with outdoor kitchen and dining area, fire pit, and running water. A cast-iron cover keeps the ashes and wood dry in the fire pit between uses. *Courtesy Town and Country Cedar Homes*

A commanding nook for dining overlooks a pretty property. *Courtesy of Green Planet Landscaping*

Stone and concrete combine for appealing effect in outdoor furnishings. *Courtesy of Green Planet Landscaping*

Photography by Keith Frederick, Environmental Landscape Associates Inc.

A flagstone patio and pergola define a modern outdoor living space with kitchen and dining for eight. *Courtesy of Environmental Landscape Associates Inc.*

Photography by Keith Frederick, Environmental Landscape Associates Inc.

Courtyard Living

In regions of the Mediterranean, an enclosed courtyard is part of practically every home. Enclosed by way of the outer walls, that is. The goal is a private space left open to the sky. Here are two examples of courtyard spaces, both outfitted with a fireplace to create a living room out of doors.

A romantic courtyard, accented in rich autumn tones, is illuminated by a bee-hive-style fireplace that sparkles in one corner. *Courtesy Toll Brothers, Inc.*

Stone columns define a stately courtyard, with a towering chimney forming a centerpiece and electronic entertainment another fiery draw. *Courtesy Eldorado Stone*

Loggia & Other Home Extensions

Some might say a gas fireplace outside is cheating, but it's so convenient! Few would figure out that the stone isn't real—it's a manufactured stone veneer that can fool the most discerning eye. *Courtesy Eldorado Stone*

Again, borrowing from Mediterranean tradition, the loggia is a covered room open to the outdoors and protected from the elements above by a floor of the home. In the Mediterranean regions, these rooms gain architectural appeal, their roofs supported by columns and framed by arches. However, the idea of outdoor rooms as an extension of the home takes on many forms in today's home designs. Here is an exploration of such rooms, outfitted for cooking and high living.

A grill unit sits within a semicircular stage area, with a stretch of countertop beyond where friends and family can sample tidbits fresh from the flames. *Courtesy Toll Brothers, Inc.*

Beams crisscross, creating an imaginary ceiling over this complete outdoor kitchen. A terracotta floor and furnishings bring a homey ambiance outside in a climate where being outdoors is more often inviting than not. *Courtesy of Mid Continent Cabinetry*

A big, stucco fireplace in warm stucco hues adds Tuscan-style to this outdoor kitchen, where a wall of very contemporary appliances shelters under the overhang of the home. *Courtesy of Reynolds Gualco Architecture-Interior Design*

A tiled arch forms a backdrop for a loggia kitchen, tucked behind a spiral staircase.
Courtesy of Green Planet Landscaping

Open-air cooking takes place poolside, while a log-gia helps defend loungers from excessive sunlight. *Courtesy Toll Brothers, Inc.*

A fireplace caps the end of a loggia, furnished like a sitting room, Southwestern style. *Courtesy Toll Brothers, Inc.*

A massive chimney rises like a natural formation through the roof of this log home, built
of locally harvested fieldstone in keeping
with a patio wall. *Courtesy of Hearthstone, Inc.*

A mantel and moldings create classic Colonial ambiance for this sheltered fireplace.
Courtesy of Facings of America

A fireplace, built directly on the side of the home, adds allure to an outside room. *Courtesy Toll Brothers, Inc.*

With full formal dining room, a huge fireplace, carpeting, ceiling fan, and chandeliers, an experience in this loggia is one to remember! *Courtesy of Reynolds Gualco Architecture-Interior Design*

Photography by Dave Adams Photography

Pavilions & Pergolas

If your region gets rain, or blistering sun, a backyard room is infinitely more useful when it has a roof. Pavilions provide open-air rooms with a full roof, and usually make a pretty focal point for the backyard. Likewise, pergolas are architecturally appealing, though their slatted roofs are purely for protection against sun. In both cases, these structures provide a framework for a gathering, creating a niche within a broader landscape where people migrate and mingle.

Photography by Roger Wade Studio

Stone and log form the framework for an outdoor room, with kitchen facilities, dining area, and a wood-fired furnace. *Courtesy Town and Country Cedar Homes*

A clever outdoor kitchen design uses a partial wall to create a natural screen, along with a dramatic arched entryway. Within, an intimate area for dining, and relaxing takes place under a log pole ceiling. *Courtesy of Sundancer Creations*

Photography by Snap It

A contemporary pavilion forms the perimeter for a spacious outdoor kitchen. *Courtesy of Patio Pools & Spas*

A covered outdoor kitchen offers a focal point for entertaining—and cooking!
Courtesy of Green Scene Landscape

An extension of the home, a pergola overshadows a cooking center, while furnishings
establish gathering spots to dine and digest. *Courtesy Toll Brothers, Inc.*

A tile-roofed pavilion shelters an outdoor kitchen, where guests are welcomed to
dine and relax poolside. *Courtesy of Patio Pools & Spas*

Photography by Mary B. Vail, OSG Publicist

The stone pavilion creates an elegant outdoor poolside living room. *Courtesy of Paragon Pools*

Wrought iron caps a pagoda framing a fireplace, creating an airy evening retreat. *Courtesy of Green Scene Landscape*

A fireplace forms the jewel within the setting of a beautiful pavilion. *Courtesy Toll Brothers, Inc.*

41

River stones clad a chimney and the log columns of a beautiful pavilion.
Courtesy Town and Country Cedar Homes

An exciting outdoor dining experience begins with a classic pavilion
complemented by sculptured brick
and wrought iron accents. *Courtesy
Menefee & Winer Architects*

45

This cozy setting for outdoor dining and relaxing reiterates that, "There's no place like home." *Courtesy Menefee & Winer Architects*

Sunken Patios

Whether conquering an uneven terrain, or adding interest to a very flat one, sunken patios are a wonderful way to define a living space outdoors. Moreover, the walls inherent in a sunken patio make perfect built-in seating and, in some cases, countertop. These images also explore some innovative inset rooms that allow cooks and bartenders to cozy up close to a pool or deck area.

This little round retreat is a neighborhood delight, with circular bench seating that invites everyone to move in close to the action. *Courtesy of Green Planet Landscaping*

Photography by Mary B. Vail, OSG Publicist

A sunken outdoor kitchen serves as a swimmers' bar, the perfect way to interact with guests as they lounge in the pool! *Courtesy of Paragon Pools*

A fireplace surround embraces an intriguing sunken patio, forming an inner circle within a larger patio environment. *Courtesy of Environmental Landscape Associates Inc.*

Multiple levels add charm and intrigue to a patio and deck. Tucked under the rail, a cook center enjoys a nice tiled countertop, as well as the capstone surfaces that finish the walls framing a sunken patio and a raised fireplace patio that sits flush with the deck. *Courtesy of Environmental Landscape Associates Inc.*

A sunken kitchen creates an intimate spot,
with elevated seating to overlook the pool.
Courtesy of Patio Pools & Spas

Photography by Snap It

Photography by Mary B. Vail, OSG Publist

An inviting pool bar at the edge of the outdoor kitchen encourages swimmers and loungers alike to put in their orders! *Courtesy of Paragon Pools*

Photography by Mary B. Vail, OSG Publist

A sunken outdoor kitchen incorporates a touch of romance, with stringed lights and wispy curtains. The swim-up bar provides an opportunity for refreshments while luxuriating in the cool waters of the pool. *Courtesy of Paragon Pools*

Walled Patios

An alternative to going sub-terrain with a patio is to raise up walls around it. In an urban setting, or a windy one, these walls provide a level of privacy and protection. In most cases, any view worth enjoying is still there when you stand up. Moreover, the walls themselves become part of the view, whether adorned or stunningly designed.

Stucco is a wonderful substance, freeing the imagination to form curves and characters and unifying nearly any imaginable surface. *Courtesy of Patio Pools & Spas*

Two warm tones unify fireplace, walls, and hearth. *Courtesy of Patio Pools & Spas*

Photography by Snap It

This outdoor kitchen features every indoor convenience—refrigeration, cooling drawers and duel grills for cooking. To keep everyone cozy during gatherings, an outdoor fireplace takes the chill out of the cool air. *Courtesy of Paragon Pools*

Photography by Mary B. Vail, OSG Publicist

Vibrant colors, pink and blue, seem perfect in a Southwestern setting where cool nights lend themselves to a little fire. *Courtesy of Patio Pools & Spas*

Lighting enhances a greatroom, where kitchen, dining, and living spaces collide for delightful entertaining outdoors. *Courtesy of Green Planet Landscaping*

Photography by Eryn Ence
Designs by Damon Lang and Green Planet Landscaping

A pergola crowns the rise of a chimney and shelters the fireplace and bench seats. *Courtesy of Patio Pools & Spas*

A beehive fireplace invites loungers to this gated-patio haven. *Courtesy of Sundancer Creations*

51

Stone forms a countertop and rustic backsplash amidst a stucco and stainless steel kitchen setting. *Courtesy Joyce Hoshall Interiors*

Photography by Mary B. Vail, OSG Publist

The authentic Mexican-style pizza oven takes center stage in a well-outfitted outdoor kitchen. *Courtesy of Paragon Pools*

Photography by Mary B. Vail, OSG Publist

A beautiful stone oven finishes off a stretch of outdoor kitchen poolside. Countertop in front of a wood-fired oven is very useful as you manipulate combustibles and comestibles in and out of a very hot space. *Courtesy of Los Angeles Ovenworks*

A stately cook center, Spanish style, beckons at the far edge of an expansive patio. *Courtesy Toll Brothers, Inc.*

An outdoor bar allows the host to serve friends and family in style. *Courtesy of Patio Pools & Spas*

A pergola filters light to a handsome adobe kitchen. Its column supports accent the wrap-around design of the cooking and food preparation areas. *Courtesy of Green Planet Landscaping*

Slate caps a stretch of outdoor counter, complete with plumbed sink and a fire-ring for stir fry. *Courtesy of Green Planet Landscaping*

Cut flagstone pieces cap a peninsular counter atop a stone kitchen surround that culminates in a dramatic, three-tiered fireplace surround. Walled enclosures around a backyard can make outdoor living space more intimate and insulated from sound and wind. *Courtesy of Green Planet Landscaping*

A sensational outdoor kitchen and fire space can entertain in any number of ways—from splashing in a sunny swimming pool by day, to a perfectly grilled dinner at sunset, followed by a flickering fire late at night! *Courtesy of Green Planet Landscaping*

What better way to cook and entertain than overlooking a grand swimming pool! Look in another direction, and one can see the countryside beyond. Unlike rooms defined by walls, outdoor rooms embrace the views. *Courtesy of Green Planet Landscaping*

Lounge by the pool, chat by the fire, or cook in the spectacular kitchen in this outdoor setting nestled within a neighborhood of homes. *Courtesy of Green Planet Landscaping*

Positively musical, this themed outdoor kitchen offers elegant furnishings and colorful details—a welcome invitation to any guest. *Courtesy of Green Planet Landscaping*

Photography by Keith Frederick,
Environmental Landscape Associates Inc.

Photography by Keith Frederick,
Environmental Landscape Associates Inc.

A full-size outdoor kitchen shelters under a gorgeous wooden pergola, supported by beautiful stone columns. Images taken by day and night show the virtues and versatility of a food-prep area that includes a wok unit, grill, and steaming trays, among other amenities. *Courtesy of Environmental Landscape Associates Inc.*

Photography by Keith Frederick,
Environmental Landscape Associates Inc.

Photography by Keith Frederick,
Environmental Landscape Associates Inc.

This outdoor kitchen and cabana is sleek with a split-level bar and granite
countertop. *Courtesy Southwest Tile and Marble*

Design by Fanny Bolen Interiors
Photography by Amy McCollom of Southwest Tile & Marble
Contracted by Bailey Contracting

Fire Pits

A circle of fire evokes our most primitive human gathering. The flickering fire is mesmerizing, its warmth a magnet. The comfort of fire lowers blood pressure, and allows friends and family to relax. People look great in a fire's glow, and feel at ease with flames to stare at.

Relaxing around burning embers is the ideal way to spend an evening. *Courtesy of Green Planet Landscaping*

A backyard campground setting reflects the fun-loving nature of the owners, who freely offer these spacious guest accommodations to friends. A fire pit is the focal point of the fun for a family that likes to move the action out of doors. *Courtesy of Golden Eagle Log Homes*

Manufacturers are falling over themselves to create products that make it easy for people to have the comfort of open fire in places where firewood, and local ordinances, might make the proposition prohibitive. Here's an example of a wonderful gas unit, easily turned on and off. It is shown here surrounded with real stone—the unit is at home in any natural environment. *Courtesy of Napoleon Fireplaces & Grills*

83

Courtesy of Green Planet Landscaping

Park bench seating and a fire pit create an illusion of camping in the heart of the forest. *Courtesy of Realm Designs, Inc.*

Photography by Morris Gindi

Photography by Roger Wade Studio

A lakefront lot gets added amenities with a decorative concrete patio and built-in fire pit. *Courtesy Town and Country Cedar Homes*

A small space celebrates the four elements: earth, fire, water, and sky, framed by a colorful tiled half wall. *Courtesy of Green Planet Landscaping*

Water and fire against a natural rock formation bring the best of the great outdoors to a small space. *Courtesy of Green Planet Landscaping*

A fire pit marks the dramatic terminus of a zero-edge swimming pool. *Courtesy of Sundancer Creations*

Comfy chairs encircle a fire pit, arranged on a permeable expanse of lawn and oversize paver stones. More "formal" dining takes place under an expansive pergola nearby. *Courtesy of Sundancer Creations*

Courtesy of Sundancer Creations

Firelight romanticizes any evening. *Courtesy of Patio Pools & Spas*

A fire pit was built-in to bench seating. *Courtesy of Patio Pools & Spas*

Photography by Snap It

Stone caps a fire pit, its circular shape repeated in the spa/fountain beyond. *Courtesy of Patio Pools & Spas*

Tie wires secure grape vines and flowering vines to traverse the perimeters of this fire pit and patio. In the meantime, it's an opportunity to catch a glimpse of a site that will soon be privately enjoyed. *Courtesy of Paragon Pools*

Photography by Mary B. Vail, Publicist

A western-themed fire pit beckons brightly in the center of an elevated patio. *Courtesy of Paragon Pools*

Photography by Mary B. Vail, OSG Publicist

A dramatic slash of fire culminates a semi-circular patio. The colorful pillows add interest and comfortable allure to the awe-inspiring setting. *Courtesy of Green Planet Landscaping*

Impressive duel WetFlames®, combination fire and water features, cast a warm glow over a pool area. *Courtesy of Paragon Pools*

Numberous fireballs and torches add a warm glow to the Oriental-themed palapa and setting. *Courtesy of Paragon Pools*

Photography by Mary B. Vail, OSG Publicist

This sunken fire pit with circular seating forms a cozy conversation nook. *Courtesy of Paragon Pools*

Photography by Mary B. Vail, OSG Publicist

A fire pit leaps to life at the turn of a knob, providing nighttime illumination and allure to an already inviting pool and raised spa. *Courtesy of Paragon Pools*

Fire forms the divide between pool and spa, set within the rambling environment of a backyard. *Courtesy Toll Brothers, Inc.*

Poolside seating includes a built-in bench that encircles a matching fire pit. *Courtesy of Green Planet Landscaping*

This fire pit illustrates how the age-old appeal of outdoor fire can be adapted to modern sensibilities. *Courtesy of Green Planet Landscaping*

Iron and stone take on innovative form for a fire pit in the foreground, while equal creativity went into the design of a sun-worshipping altar just beyond. *Courtesy Toll Brothers, Inc.*

Fireplaces

One of the hottest new trends in the back-yard is the outdoor fireplace. Whether added as an extension of the home, or situated at a far corner of the patio, a lit fireplace acts as a party magnet. By day, these sculptural masterpieces form a focal point in the yard and an irresistible attraction.

Photography by Keith Frederick, Environmental Landscape Associates Inc.

A fireplace forms the center of an arched triptych.
Courtesy of Environmental Landscape Associates Inc.

Photography by Keith Frederick, Environmental Landscape Associates Inc.

Retaining walls form wonderful bench seats for this sunken patio, should the inviting chairs become full. Fire, as well as a portable outdoor heater, extend the season for this outdoor room.
Courtesy of Environmental Landscape Associates Inc.

Adobe construction contributes to the Spanish-revival flair of fireplaces with clean lines and geometric details. Constructed in varied sizes, these designs fit equally well on small or large patios.
Courtesy of Green Planet Landscaping

With the look and feel of a Tuscan home, this outdoor kitchen and fireplace is perfect for romantic dining and relaxed living. *Courtesy of Environmental Landscape Associates Inc.*

Courtesy of Green Planet Landscaping

Courtesy of Green Scene Landscape

A stylish stone fireplace is stunning on this elevated patio, crowned with a pergola. Right next door, an outdoor kitchen includes a buffet-sized counter-top and appliances. *Courtesy of Green Scene Landscape*

This wood-fired oven incorporates two compartments for storing wood. *Courtesy of Green Planet Landscaping*

A brick fireplace adds antique ambiance to a backyard, flanked by cushions that make cozying up to the fire quite inviting. *Courtesy Joyce Hoshall Interiors*

Pretty accessories personalize this outdoor setting, adding pretty to a handsome stone fireplace capped by clay chimneys. *Courtesy of Green Planet Landscaping*

A beautiful stone tower fireplace creates a focal feature for this back-yard entertainment area. *Courtesy of Green Planet Landscaping*

A towering fireplace forms a functional folly in the garden, made handsome with stone and stucco finish. *Courtesy of Green Planet Landscaping*

A slatted pergola adds to the comfort and tranquility of outdoor dining. *Courtesy of Green Planet Landscaping*

Mosaic tile brings excitement to fireside relaxation. *Courtesy of Green Planet Landscaping*

A stone wall feels like an organic outcropping, and forms a beautiful barrier wall and fire chamber for this stylish patio. *Courtesy Joyce Hoshall Interiors*

This magnificent fireplace is a virtual light show: the staggered rise surround is perfect for a lanterns and candles display, and blue glass teams with gas for a different firelight effect below. *Courtesy of Green Planet Landscaping*

A stately brick fireplace brings traditional and civility to the campfire. *Courtesy of Green Scene Landscape*

A fireplace provides a spectacular attraction at the far side of a pool. *Courtesy Toll Brothers, Inc.*

Fire and water create two walls of this courtyard-like space. *Courtesy Toll Brothers, Inc.*

Rustic stacked stone trims a pool edge and frames a corner fireplace and bench seating. *Courtesy of Green Scene Landscape*

Photography by Snap It

The extended walls and hearth of the fireplace seem to embrace visitors. *Courtesy of Patio Pools & Spas*

Outside feels like in, with a spacious fireplace and upholstered furnishings. *Courtesy Toll Brothers, Inc.*

A sculptural fireplace adds adornment to a long vista. *Courtesy of Patio Pools & Spas*

A beehive fireplace sits pretty within a twilight landscape. *Courtesy of Patio Pools & Spas*

A fireplace doubles as outdoor sculpture, handsomely installed on a patio pedestal. *Courtesy of Patio Pools & Spas*

Photography by Snap It

A beehive fireplace sits at the outer radius of a circular cobblestone patio. *Courtesy of Patio Pools & Spas*

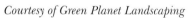
Courtesy of Green Planet Landscaping

Outdoors lovers revel in a winter wonderland, sheltered by a pavilion roof and warmed by a big stone fireplace. *Courtesy Town and Country Cedar Homes*

Photography by Keith Frederick, Environmental Landscape Associates Inc.

There's something to be said for outdoor cooking by a great fireplace! *Courtesy of Environmental Landscape Associates Inc.*

A handsome stone fireplace is flanked by hearthside-seating. *Courtesy of Green Planet Landscaping*

Courtesy of Green Planet Landscaping

Whether basking by the fire or relaxing in the wood and brick design, this
outdoor fire scene offers quaint tranquility. *Courtesy of Neely Design Associates*

Resource Guide

The following contributors are go-to experts and suppliers when you're planning your backyard environment. Be sure to check out their websites to learn more about them.

Conrad Imports, Inc.
San Francisco, California
866-426-6723
www.conradshades.com

Eldorado Stone
San Marcos, California
800-925-1491
www.eldoradostone.com

Environmental Landscape Assoc. Inc.
Doylestown, Pennsylvania
800-925-9252
www.elaontheweb.com

Facings of America
Phoenix, Arizona
602-955-9217
www.facingsofamerica.com

Green Planet Landscaping
Las Vegas, Nevada
702-614-8866
www.greenplanetlandscaping.com

Green Scene Landscape
Canoga Park, California
818-227-0740
www.greenscenelandscape.com

Golden Eagle Log Homes
Wisconsin Rapids, Wisconsin
800-270-5025
www.goldeneagleloghomes.com

Hearthstone, Inc.
Dandridge, Tennessee
800-247-4442
www.hearthstonehomes.com

Joyce Hoshall Interiors
Folsom, California
916-765-7538
www.hoshallsfolsom.com

Los Angeles Ovenworks
Los Angeles, California
800-516-5716
www.losangelesovenworks.com

Menefee & Winer Architects
Atlanta, Georgia
404-876-0793
www.menefeeandwiner.com

Mid Continent Cabinetry
Eagan, Minnesota
651-234-3344
www.midcontinentcabinetry.com

Napoleon Appliance Corporation
Barrie, Ontario, Canada
888-726-2220
www.napoleongrills.com

Neely Design Associates
Atlanta, Georgia
(404) 817-0807

Paragon Pools
Las Vegas, Nevada
702-251-0500
www.paragonpools.net

Patio Pools & Spas
Tucson, Arizona
1-800-my-patio6
www.patiopoolsaz.com

Realm Designs, Inc.
Warren, New Jersey
908-753-3939
www.realmdesignsinc.com

Reynolds Gualco
Sacramento, California
916-456-3720
www.rgaid.com

Southwest Tile & Marble
Oklahoma City, Oklahoma
405-235-3393
www.swt.com

Sundancer Creations
Santa Fe, New Mexico
505-470-4365
www.sundancercreations.com

Toll Brothers, Inc.
Horsham, Pennsylvania
215-938-8000
www.tollbrothers.com

Town & Country Cedar Homes
Petoskey, Michigan
800-9683178
www.cedarhomes.com